Book for
Lonely Evenings

Book for
Lonely Evenings

Ethan R. Ray

RESOURCE *Publications* • Eugene, Oregon

BOOK FOR LONELY EVENINGS

Resource Publications
An Imprint of Wipf and Stock Publishers
199 W. 8th Ave., Suite 3
Eugene, OR 97401

www.wipfandstock.com

PAPERBACK ISBN: 978-1-6667-0051-0
HARDCOVER ISBN: 978-1-6667-0052-7
EBOOK ISBN: 978-1-6667-0053-4

04/27/21

Contents

Beginning of the Book

Tired like a dirty saloon

The unchecked footsteps of a forestalled noon
Brought you like a ritual to the return of the grappling

Peanut shells and green broken glass along the pleated crease of
    your remembrance
Of that place, of that dream a-wandering

It filled the floor and all you could think of was the silent dashing
    of wind against your
Childhood memories and middle agedness clocked by the swing-
    miss of the American
Strike out

You stuck out like a sore butcher looking for his clothes in the
    cattle ground, looking just
Like
The man in a painting of a ranch from another century, and the
    butcher awkwardly reminding
Himself

Of his duty

You cried at the front of the classroom, and somehow you were
    beginning to be brought back

To the wicked days of gray sky elementary school, with the weird
     cigarette butt in your
Back pack and the sheer madness of wanting to be alone

I don't think it's so ridiculous to want to be away from it all, is
     what I wish she would have said

But back to the main point, back to the focus of our discussion,
     back to the beginning of the book

Back to death, back to back

The saloon was really just a steakhouse in a forlorn town and
     neither of your parents drank and
You felt like it was sickening the way the peanut shells under-
     neath crinkled to your

Fourth grade sneaker, and the loud smoking section, back when
     they had them but you didn't
Know what smoking was, and I

Bleed in the forsaken night, forgetting now where I went for those
     fifteen miles
I enter sadly into a saloon nightly and watch for bright black eyes
     and a fitting smile, because

If I can't love you, then who can I love; whose hand can I reach
     for in times like these?

Even though the butcher's duty was to the saloon in the first
     place, you still can't help but
Wonder

What happened to the diamond forest beside the sea except once
     removed so the sea is
Something you imagine in your fourth grade sneakers and the
     focus of the discussion
Was the painting

Sill

Fleece

On a hill, love.

They took down everything I gave to my family, my horse, my
cottage

So guileful and benign from my dream

I tramped down among the flowers and felt like an earthquake,
splitting

Screeching howling scratching burning sifting sewing moving
knowing leaving
Greeting solitude seeping musically weeping salutes in leaving
and a brief

Salutation from the dawn, and I was off again like a swept hilt
sword, singing.

I mimicked the dead and found that the city was a doorway

I cried and left out pieces of the sunlight from my dreaming, and
hang the rest

Put it in some portrait or fixture of light in the modern era so it
can be forgotten like

Lust, lust for a believed hush in their quiet upper room, candles
    for the room

And making signs toward the concrete, below, down, sinking, I
    know it was grief

That took you from your home, your sweated out pillow, your
    grim bits and bits of pieces

Cut from a rag that was given to you by your family, and some-
    where deep in the recesses
Of night

Was the fleece that you stuffed rapidly your pack with, against the
    lips of the ragged lamp
With

The benighted fingers of coyness, and death dropped in, left the
    newspaper on the second-story

Window

Sill

And then took some flowers to your mother, and kept secrets
    from one another, and then left

You

Silent

By a crouched wicked end line . . .

Leaves of seeped music and tea from end to end, you whispered
    to him then,

"I saw you on the promenade giving a speech to which I walked
    away quietly into a chaos night"

And the knighthood was simply another window to the moon.

Future Machine

We wake with the sun
Bedfellows, returning home
The night

I had several good conversations with people I barely knew
And they encouraged the night, the eclipsed nature of knowing
    what

In the middle of time, they were striving for

And they left and I left and I went to sleep

Why is it that sometimes you wake in the morning beautiful
And the sun is there with you, sometimes in tandem with what
    you may have dreamed

But there is a bridge between dreams and the waking, a limitless
    eclipsing of the past

Time is marriage

I know that you forgot to tell me, but it doesn't matter now

Those conversations happened without you, and now I leave this
    place, this past night
With a good face and too much dream wine

Cool morning, she said, waking

It was all a very cool time, she said, waking

I trust that you know the patterns of your heart

They light up as you are tuned to a tuning of a future-machine

That lets you show them how you think about rock and roll
That lets you show them how to make peace, but

They also know that the best way to plug into machines is to
make a song, anyway, and

Some people will understand, someday, and that brings me joy

But time is married to the truth, which is that you don't have far
to go, my friend

Not far to go to be enveloped in the bliss of silence in the

Sun-drenched January morning, when it wasn't too cold and the
light was clear and vivid

Allowing for sacred dreams to be taken up and away with the
time, taken taken away

As you cried for the past without making any movement, just
remembering

And you still search for something that's always lost, which keeps
you alive

Phonograph Sound

You thought you knew what to say
But cars pass you as you walk beside the road to some restaurant

And you forget because of some woman long ago

And you forget, and you reminisce at once, about the long hidden
     happiness

Of another tomorrow

You wanted it, you were there, and you saw it, but

You don't have it and now, you remember that art is pain and

Sitting on your bed pathetically holding a glass of grape juice, you
     think of the golden
Memory of the future

But since you can't have it, and it has passed you by, like the cars
     you watched go by you

Mercilessly
Before you walked back home to yourself, and someone else
Someone, beauty, something, love

Some hidden other future, which you carry around now in your
     pocket

And think of it from time to time, listening to music

Which has softness in the corners of the room sometimes, but
    only in a black shade of the
Evening

I don't care how much it would have taken you now, because I
    know it wasn't

Me that would sit at a comfortable place and have the laughter of
    children

In the garden

My days go by and I wonder, just only wonder
At that time I never had

Autumn leaves too quickly and I can't always find the death mo-
    tions as wonderful as
They should be, so I take a walk

With my friend moonlight
With my friend night
And I feel the empty faces

I know what you feel like, forlorn faces, I know, I know

There once was a time for you

But beckoning down the road are some pirates which I see and
    am filled
With necessary joy to join them

But for a moment am reluctant to leave the narrow hidden rail-
    road street

Behind me, even though it was made long ago and I can't
    remember

How it was made

And then several of my past lights go out, and I put them on
    ships and send them away

Send them away like messages, like words one that doesn't know
    me will see sometime
On a book with paper, and they won't understand

Just how small a town can be
And just how much they won't know about

What it was to make those sculptures which are
Hiding around in the corners of the phonograph sound

And like medicine taken from a stranger I disembark

From the path, and go away with them.

Hawaii Rob

Puckered pinching nerves
Sticking to skull tapes
Wishing hoping worms
Lost rite anecdote

Slow clammed smoke
And when he wrote
It broke and smote
His favorite hero Quixote

So that when pew'd
He confessed

His heaven was a formless mess of

Quickly rotting bones

And when he gave
Along his grave
A mountain of sand which turned him away

Put a question in a nickel and give it
So said he.

Eternal Is My Kiss

I blundered forth in the darkened myth
Go with, he said, be quick
The preacher with his demon fork
Be quick, he said, don't miss
The eternal rhyming of a soul
Through a window-pane of languished old
And beside the thousand music fold
A chord he said, behold

What clearer truth can you expunge
For the mystic eye of Satan's wrung
What callous thoughts can wind be-sung
Go with, he said, be quick

An Irish eye for conniver's lie
Don't miss, he said, be quick
I've blessed you with the demon eye
And a kiss, be quick

Before the rhythm do you miss
At the handle of the dark
At the rotunda of the mark
And the believing of the night
What it brings, my love
Be quick with your civic sight
And do not forget the wisdom might
Of the night, he said, be quick

He turned to me and with the sea
Destroyed the wondering light
And brought forth, with truth
The love of ancient blackened tunes
Of myth, he said, be quick

I bleed
The light
Is gone
I fright

And the spell awakes, my soul forsakes to the dark
Don't miss, he said, be quick

And what you do miss
Of that I say this
Eternal is my kiss
Be quick, my friend, be quick

Robert Two-Hands

Look beneath my pale face
And you will see
A monster snarl and be-gnarl
The quick and light, you see.

In my right hand

Lightning

In my left

Death

The left side of my face
Is a burnt piece of flesh
That through a pore of eternity
Might flinch at fire

And through the soreness of other heart
Is ten millionth the degree
Of sooted willow bark

It rests there, a callous
That no heavenly arrow
Can pierce the marrow
Of my bones hardened

By fire

I feel its gray self color
Harden at its brother
The right side of my face
The peaked heaven-color.

Leave

What meaning have you for me
Who sits in the rain station of love
Who deciphers some coded ancient being
Who never takes responsibility for Fake

Light is not warm to you
Your name is secret
You bury bones still alive in dwellings beneath souls
And you fervently chip away pieces of being

I am not a martyr
I want to go with you, wonderful people
I want to see where you live and drink your strange drinks
I want to love you

But you do not take me with you and I am

Stranded

Believe what I give to you
It is little more than nothing
It is what I call home
It is insanity

It is a dusted blinded rhyme
Saved forever by those bedroom crawling chocolate lovers

That I understand so well

I want to get out
I want to show you that I am wonderful but I am little
More than a beggar at your door

You do not care because I make up in my mind that you do not

Care

And that itself is good enough for me

So I take knives and throw them at portraits

Of my past loves and I decide

That this was loving them more than I could have ever done

Go

The blue lights rescinded
But I saw between them
The glow of the skeleton of mirth
Ragged and young, crying "go"

And I smiled and I didn't follow
I walked the other direction
Into an ocean of peace

Beside the Church's Bells

Alongside your endless road
You pick and cradle your flowers
And you never pay heed to what you're told
About them wilting within the hour

So you stuff them, one by one
Inside your brilliant basket
You wonder and you pray
That there will be a time for them

There once was a love
That glimmered deep in dark
It shone its many wonders
To those that it chose

And with a sudden violent crying
It showed you it was dying
And took you to a place where you were lying
Beside the church's bells

How many years will you wonder
What happened to your flowers
How bright and calm the sea is
In your waking sorrow

Crude cruel callus
Around your once-bold eye
Shows you the parting of the sky
Along the horizons you can't see

No one knows
When the times will change
No one can make cease
The wonderful, bleeding, forgotten feeling

The quick potent light
Of a new life begins
And I wonder, still and quiet
Where I have been

I try to put before you
All those golden days
That I played music for my maker
Freedom was his name

Yet all I can do is this
Ask you a question
What happened to your songs
That I used to play?

There once was a city
That I could call my home
There once was a city
Beside the sound of her voice

I take with me now
Not too soft, and not too gently
The makeshift corners of life
Into a bed of flowers

And what you will find

Ends softly with your name

Written in the Barley Street Tavern

The young men scramble and the old men pray
That there will be a time for them

But they ascend the same stair
Daylight beware of their dreaming friend

The old gate may open and find just a joke
But the same friends always return
And the lusting battery of heaven will disappear

Find your old favorite rhythm and don't return
Don't leave the shapes or the dying songs

But find a train to bring you along

The station is your wounded heart
From which the flying demons spark.

And the same refrain is monstrous
It returns again
But you wish it away

The day is gone and the people
Wish for justice

The king gives it and it
Belongs again

To the night

Tigress

Combine in your heart
The ways that are true
Coalesce in you
Your deepest love

And remind yourself again
That it was nothing to do with you
But rather, churches are always silent
In the morning forgotten

And yes, I can tell you
That there will be a time
When you can witch away old mistakes

That clamber and chop

Atop a faked sunrise
Which you know you shouldn't see

I have
For you
An ancient tune
A locking away of the tigress

But you would never want it, you would never see

That old playful killing that lingers with me

Something you wished for long ago
Something you wanted to know
Something is breaking the day away
And finding you're awake

My Blessed Virgin

My blessed virgin
Who has not seen the
Glorious bursting
Of a thousand voices
Of heaven be sucked
Into the velvet chasm of
Peace does not know
That when my darkness,
Warm and mysterious in my kiss
Shrouds them with a cocoon
Of the kind of love that
Breaks hearts, that
I am pouring myself
Into their soul

And they break it
Break it like the bow
Of Odysseus's ship on
A lost window of hope

You cannot take my
Darkness

It Is Not What You Think It Is

I walked upon the midnight sound
Of the lament of the chosen
And within the walls of broken calls
I found the reflection

I found it lost and kept alive
By the very breath that it was denied
By the ending page that it designed
The secret tangle of longing

When you go out and feel them grow
When you move about and find it
When you know that what it was comes now
To your bliss, then bind it

Bind fields of wishing on your own
Build locks and chests and lockets
Bring tools that you knew could be
The end of your returning

But do not wait, and please don't take
Too much time in moving quickly
Because there is a place for you to wait
Inside the corners of the tide

It is the night, so sweet and bright
So gifted in your sorrow
It is the way in which the day
Brings down its shades of tomorrow

It is not what
You think it is
It is not a place or thing

It is the feeling that
Abides in you

It is the way you sing

Communing with the Nation

Communing with the nation
Is feeding mathematical information to a painter
And watching the righteous blooming of the scarred faces
Put together a time machine

I do not know where the words mean anything
Do they here anymore?
There is a call from somewhere
Yet it's the past that speaks

Volumes of itching crypts
Sing violently from the past
Yet today is lost from the beacons of yesterday

I make, I wake, I take your soul
And with rummages through this old field
I believe

What does this mean
Said the beggar

What Has Put You on a Cloud

I am afraid because
I cannot find out what this carnivorous soldier wants at my door
I am frightened by its silence

Silence is a word
But it means to live without them

I am never its master

Is there something I can do for you?
But you drink drinks tonight, and I watch you
In my mind in a far away curtain

Sorrowfully sip the satin song
Which you always knew would bring me along
Which you always understand is how I belong

To the naked biting upended throng

I have a match here in my hand
I have a batch of your broken minds
I have a handle here which interrupts time

That I can pull at your choosing

I am against everything that you spit
From your mouth

Rage and desist away the feeling of bliss that I control with a kiss
Of the night

Contain and reminisce the existence of this belligerent and coy
Rhyme of the maker

Forlorn and lost angels come weeping to your door and I wonder
aloud

What has put you on a cloud

These women, alien creatures who want to suck my soul

Out of my mouth before they destroy it so

Then I lose control and

Shut the door.

Suspicion

There was a well-oiled ghost
Stomping through the field of your
Long lost lover-mother

And quailing deep and looking sweet
For the designation of tomorrow

And the throes of two people
Friends who were assumed lovers
Dashed bliss against a violet
Wave of cloud like

Jupiter in December

And they spoke frequently
And dusted off the snowflakes
Which they kept for the wreck
Of the scraping sorrow
They found inside a rhythm

Of hope

That there could be that
Garden where Muses spoke
About their minds.

There is no place two friends
Can go where
As they chase after black dewdrops

That can be safe from

A beguiling sinner called

Suspicion

Eye

You can see within the bleeding fire
Trust, wait and taste within
The single joy that burns desire
Scrawled with skeleton pin

A match, it wanes, purple feign
Of what imbues this sacred watch
This clock of lungs, this gross tongue
I watched you with my left eye
Hole in right and battered wrung

Black and blithe a baneful botch
Of your shapeless desert smock

And took you, helpless and foul-breathed
Into rotten, gray frozen chalk
And made thee my writing block.

But sever for me, then
Your bones and your legs, then
I'll show you who to kiss

To connive eternal bliss

It is the crow who every day
With one eye fades away
The dream you had this day

In the pit.

Instructions

It was some day in the middle of the dungeon
When a sun-cracked voice took it upon itself to declare

Everything invisible

There are some times when pieces of a ship nail themselves to
   walls, in
A permanence
Only broken by the voice

And then they call out in a dreadful tone, making no sound and
   they
Sweep themselves off their feet and call to a new home

I can see the way your mouth moves in the dark
I can see the swelling might of the endless mark
I can begin to breathe out the works that you chose in your heart

I can show you what love is

But tomorrow is so quick, it frustrates the divers diving
The pipers piping, the raging fire of a trash bin in the bright alley
   surrounded
By those old names that used to be shelved next to your ashes, but
In this decree, in this trap that you've laid for me, you've given me

Instructions

On how to destroy myself with words

Rhythms

The cadence of the night, and by some magic

By some glance of hand and face, you bring me to my knees, and
everything

You spoke at another place where the sun was shining and your
hair was like the sea

You trapped me, and now that I know that every wish that I make
of love

Every sacred beginning

Is doomed like the beginning of a new day where some child
seeks a magic invisible place
Where young princes without faces bring to bear their lighted
torches and kill

Monsters in mirrors.

Fire

Courage was the best emotion

Sit sometime by the books that you bought
And be with them

Courage was the best emotion

When the wrapping-paper of the final gifts that you gave
Were tossed aside and then given up to the fire
Then you made a heart-pattern out of the dying embers

Which did not smoke

Finally place your last name on the card
And walk in a file, step to and fro
Against the blooming wreckage of the people
Who put you there
And kindle again something grotesque
So that you may find it later, and rejoice
So that you may

In time, be joyful

Blessed are the choked stories which crumble at your hand
When you put them away
Blessed are the flowers that you said could stay
And dress them up in the finest embers

Dress them for the end

Sometimes a dark clay light from the broken night
And the festival with the hanging lights suspended several times
In the air

Give you a sense that the mirror that you put in the tower that
    destroys the tithes of

Smoke that

Suspended everything in the air, this invisible blue

When you felt that she could come near you

Again there is a watching letter, again there is a method better

For which to describe your feeble feeling

That she gave to you once through your head
That she gave to you when you said goodbye

And nothing comes to you then, in the dying fire

Of your crackling whisper love

In the hushed hills lit by candles, in the bludgeoning wind you
    wish you
Could have made.

Written While Waiting for Friends

If I stay awake too long

And fill my days with friends
Then the morning will be on the mend from your gesture

The beginning

Repairing damaged days that you whispered in grace
In the darkness

But the grace left you talking again

Fill my head and my feet with the water and listen to

The beating it makes when it falls into the place you left

When you stayed awake

Changing visages, begin begin begin

Destroy it when you stand up from your sleeping place, now
Break what you take from a bowl of deepness

Beside

The voice that told you to move

And repeated are the strands that you broke

Again revenge spits out like a fountain of dreams

And culminates in the dark

Paper lanterns by a shore
Filling the same dock you filled
In ending

Leave you stranded in the vacancy of sound made
By your sleeping, which interrupted

Chains of grace from bygone days

In a pool of sky-stung, quick light fogged mountaintop

Wreathed by the silver sounds of nothing.

Virtuous Dead

What cry without
The inside wreathed machine
Can you bring for me
Can you bring for me

I need to decide
Beside the tempest dreaming

What it is you want

Virtuous dead
Solemnly dress
A breaking blast
Of the toast to the best that you knew would bless
The final quaking of the mess
That you made for me

I can glisten, I can grow
I can tell you what you already know
I can throw, I can go

Below

I wanted inside, I wanted to hide
From the faking lust of ended tide
Of breaking dust of magic cries

Of the bright mist of nothing

There watching in my face
Is the missing blessing of your grace
Is the drowning message of embraces

Too sweet to remember

Then I realize that you do not exist and I

Pack up my things like tiger rage
And I go forth in blindness
Estates are whispering at your door

They cling to the past like wishing machines
And go from the gleam into the sea

They leave the twilight without a dream

They forget to look back

Words that I do not know come before your oldness
And like the distance in a field of black

Destroy with light so quaint and other

That I can't feel it

And dismiss you for another.

Best Luck Candle

You thought of how you saw the stars for the first time
And then you came back and your sister was cursing because she
    had grown old

When you were gone

But time can be your friend when you finally realize that looking up
At the sky
Is your greatest friend

The solid masks of scorpions draw out the lingering lines between
    stars, then
And your boots which you made out of a remaining glistening
    corner of Newspaper 1913

Become your old alma mater, this chiding and sneering door
    behind where you live

Night

Day

The darlings from the parade

Commence a thousand fiends to wit them

The loving candle dripping with the chorus of your name
The walking men behind when you said the music is the same
The brilliant stabbing gutter of your lost and quiet soul
Is not the way you wanted the beginning to unfurl

Sing sing, the laughing smothered dream

And in the quiet where you poured out your innards to the
    laughing stars

There was a quiet circle of meaning around the very twines which
    bind them

Hope is the best luck candle
Walking in the dark

Again sleep like a meadow overtakes the breathing light
And as though a sacred messenger took flight in your delight
The rabid chains of waking, the deepening of love

Is something that you strove for beneath the stars above

Which, in quiet, slept you.

Chilled Smoke

The things you wrote were the things you broke
Because even though you put down some time for them

Even though you made a special consecrated place for your
    dreaming

There was not enough time for you to finish

What you started

Again there's some more days coming
And they take you over one by one in the beginning of the reel
That shows pictures on the screen, people crying, people who
    wanted

To love you

But they don't know you and will never know you and life like a
    film continues to run

Quietly your eyes grow older when you see it, for what makes age?
What makes one grow older, is it the clock on the wall or the
    number of faces

Seen

The number of faces seen in the dusty lens

You can speak a million words on seven million things
You can take some sort of car or train down to the beginning of
    your life
Where there's a river that's dried up, shadowed by broken mirrors
    and shells of you

Of

Where you've walked all your life

But you don't want to go back there, you don't want to see the
    things

Which made you

So you walk silently into the forest of the film which covers the
    passing of time
And there is no life there, only you, for a moment, only what you
    want

Because tomorrow you may see a face that you could love, but
    you will hate

It

You will come down to the meadow where they keep all of the
    cameras, and you will

Find yours, sitting beneath a tree, where no one is watching

Flickering fading notes of music bend slowly and you look
Up
At a clock

Realizing chilled smoke froze your lens

And back you go, back in

To the river which ran by your life

That you know secretly is still there, and will always be

Something to run the crackling reel as you look

Blinded, in faith

By cameras

Wound for Liars

What can you wound for the liars
Who sleep so vigorously in the shadow

Created by themselves, who cast down themselves
As they speak about it

I don't know how they got there, I told them again
I don't know you

But some time, in some way from some other place
There will be someone shining

And they will not come alight from the sky, they will not tear and
    rend
Those which made us sacred

But rather they will lie, just as you have lain

On the bed of groping musing piety.

There are designations for the people
There are mystique revelations, but they hide
And show their face only when most cruel
And destroy ties of love like tides of glory

Because if the tides come down, they will say they made them
And drown

Because honesty is a cruel curse upon the wicked
And ignorance is knowing how to move when blocked

Fathom this, again, fathom their chiding
For what makes a man, what makes a truth

Other than itself

I know what you are, you hide
But I can see where you've made the divide
It is in human heart, it is in striding down across the rivers

Where you will find that your saving has gone down into making

Nothing but the destruction of love, because in giving love you
destroy it

And the majestic piping on foreign lands only makes the love you
shake

From their hearts bleed you more, thorn-ridden martyr

Guile-less flesh
To know it is to believe in musty mutton conquer halls

Only brought to justice on a bed of fake rose glisten

And in the martyrdom lies another secret, the lie

That you felt you could hide, for so long

So long
So long

We have longed for penance, from the liar

Who dips his blade into fire

Who conquers and then expects

A child to accept his pointed death.

Bring Me My Love

Bring me my love
And let me drown
Bring my love to me

Bring me my crown
Of dust and brown
Bring my crown to me

I have not a word
For the open door
Make me a fire
To burn and sore
Make me a lantern
Of haunted yore

To make it through the door, said he.

And crown my weary face
Upon fields of deepest wonder
I left my old heart asunder
I left it with you to wonder

Will I be free?

Will I feel
That old strange feeling
Come to me with tender healing

The sound of tomorrow is not appealing
To me, said he.

And tomorrow I may leave
Upon lost autumn breeze

Tomorrow I may leave with thee.

You Could Choose To Walk on a Nicer Day

You could choose to walk on a nicer day
When the garden is green, and I am away
When the mailman brings not pain, but joy
When the children are laughing

You could choose to walk on a nicer day
When the child in my mind asks you to stay
Amongst the pillars and the halls that we made
That now are crumbling away

When the fire from the end of the world
Is a charm that you can wear
Around your neck, around your ocean eyes
Coy and mysteriously watching

When the birds stop singing their lonely song
For a moment, in which all is wrong
And giving to you that crisp piece of paper
That I wrote and you threw away

You had become my temple, my Olympus
There was no beggar of love between us
And in between ghosts of another life
I sit and sleep all day

You could choose to walk on a nicer day
When my love is not broken and gray
Like a sucked-in face covered in hope
Like a woman no one ever sees

You could choose to walk on a nicer day
Between the jade trees, and the pathway
That runs so silently away
From both of our feet, together

Yet you walk, and you kindly say
That the hills below a summer sun
Are just meaningless mounds, burial grounds
Where one can bury their dreams

But you could choose to walk on a nicer day
When the garden is green, and I am away
And there is nothing kind for you to say
Beside the hills, whispering

Plans

How long has it been
How long have you been here, my love

Staring into the chasm
Where you dropped your wedding ring

And how long my love have you stared into that chasm
In the darkness of the uncomfortable lightless night

Where you dropped down, away, around

From the sound you used to make, love

Do you know how much you feel
When you look into the reel
Do you know, have you seen
What you've done

But now it doesn't matter and there are voices from the future
that are different, now

Like the change in sun on a stark winter day, cold and bright and
far away
From the engine you designed, Plans, like their own signs

Make, make, I feel
The words you used to heal.

Inside somewhere there's a chasm
Where you dropped down
And saw as you fell
Your making

But I can't remember where I put my glasses in the morning
   sometimes and sometimes

Sometimes

I think of love

But in a way you took it, somewhere you put it, and the hourglass
   which you fought with

Has turned itself around

Look, deep, look and know
How you brought about your end
Feel, feel, I know it's real

Your pain

Again in the darkness you look down into the chasm
And somewhere you see

A face, a whisper, don't be late

A simple chord from me

And when you return in the morning and the night is all but
   forgotten

Stop and make plans to see what it means to you

On the Back of the Face of Failure

It was a cloudless blue day
And on the upper face of the totem-pole closed-up streetlight

A voice, separated, against the sky stood

Seeping an inkling of promise for the coming night
But now it's not bright and not needed

Sharing its believing in the paper-thin old skyfaring balcony
From which it blossomed

And in its face, its horror-story yearning I found some of it
Crackling through a canyon made up by nights before in my heart

The hallow breath of the Daytime Kings, the wicker screens
    brought by their fathers

The patient dreams, ripening seams the paper mounted balcony
    the real
Trees fake in the still shadowed air
Taking care to plant
Misery
In me

Then it said something through a faint distant sound you once
Found through making a lattice screen

From the top of the building, the totem-pole, the oldest rule was
    erased

And in its place a jolly face once riddled with the pockmarks of
    dreams
And a horror-story scream through the forgotten sunbeams

On the balcony of tenured dreaming

"I am an answer"

And turning its dark beams to the leaden-knighted cutting rapid
    cancers.

Your Own, After All

Smoking a bit of cigarette, you turn
Pensive in the lamplight, the burning end

Except the lamplight is the sun, and you thought about
How the sea had burned through your mind

Because the sunlight is what drives them, the cars moving below
In a place which could have been called the sea

Had you cared

But you turn gracefully and for a moment like some forgotten god
Who has since been dead, you recall some beauty that was also

Forgotten, like the time when you kissed her

I swear it's not the end
I swear
The bellowing jolly friend
Your heiress

Is the sun, and the cigarette you smoked was just a gesture against
The permanence made by the lamp, which was

After all

Your own

Because what is the world if not each heart's making

And what is the sun if not some permanent place for everyone to
    observe
The impending darkness, which makes us courageous

When we know what it will look like tomorrow when the sun

Itself

Shows us again the world, and the world

When returning

Is exactly the same

Like the time you forgot about when you kissed her, the only dif-
    ference being

In the way you love
And the burning end of the lamp
Brings you close to your sleeping place, quickly now before it burns

Out

Like the days and lives which it has always secretly known.

Forgotten Are the Bullets

A brow that is wrinkled
Does not mark the time
A person who has fought
Cannot seem to find

The beginning of a truth
Which he knew he saw quickly beneath

Bombs exploding through death

In time they will realize that no story
No matter the origin or place of existence

Can be pulled through a hole, can be subjected to whimpering
    coverings

Like water

But rather the truth like a diamond of believing comes through it
    and destroys

That old ancient mountaintop you looked so long ago for

Because it was never there
There was no one ever there atop it

Smiling and making your time

Now it is empty and the only sounds you can hear are wind-
     bursts and pieces of
Clouds filled with the grace of bitter happiness

Chiding you as you look differently at the beginning of music

Before you woke this morning, there was a sound made because
     it was an older

Sound endowed with grace, but if you continue to

Put things in bottles and jars and put them on shelves and not
     expect to find them

When you are dead

Then you are no better than a bitter sun on a day when you lose
     your love
You are no better than the beginning of time, because now at the
     end of it
At the end of your love is a beginning

I weep for the end part, because somehow it is already over

And the books you placed so carefully will fall down into the abyss
Will fall, fall eternal
If you do not pick them up now and put them apart from wires
     and clamps and disks and

Other trivial controls

Slapped in ink is a truth of soul
In the quiet morning where you heard a sound that reminded
     you how to weep

Because if you don't weep now then the barrels they took off a
    ship on Coney Island
When you came here

Are just simple nothing things that mean no more than a bed
    spread out for death

In the quiet you momentarily falter, and some candle whisks out
    like a train

And the end becomes new again, forgotten are the bullets

Forgotten are the steel cruel wind-breaking howlers which follow
    you round down

Follow you round down until your grave-time
When you become silent like mirrors of peace

I felt it again, this morning some time

A jester trying to uproot himself

Do not uproot a tree because then thousands are growing

Replenishing the piranhas and the whales

Which you could have seen if you had only stepped away from
    that door there which now
You are looking for

Good-bye, falsity, it grips
Good-bye heaven, you are needed elsewhere, you are needed
    another time

Draw in pencil your life, and you may begin to understand
That life breathes, and that when you die you are free, again, once
    now

Once ever

Were

I know that you did sleep today

I know that within the charms and the woes that bind you
You did dream stolidly without purpose

Tomorrow is the channeling of love

Another waking moment, you'll soon see
Is having to do with the ones that damned you

Is having to see that the things which bind you

Come cheerfully down through the black earth

The angle on which you stand on the earth is crooked

The angle is something that makes you go within and

You'll be alone when the world ends, I know.

Chasms of pieces of wrath
They don't form for you, they don't speak to you
They don't want you, they don't arm themselves for you

They go around your ankles and form the believed truth about
    gravity, that

It was made in the earth for you to stand crookedly

At the end you'll not move except to see God and Satan shake hands

And see the light bearer in swaddling clothes smoking a cigarette
beside the fireplace

Mansions await those with

I don't see you anymore, you don't call me on the telephone
The dreams of my youth come forth from my mouth and I speak
only of love

That gray shroud around your statuette begins to dissipate and I
know that you

Were

A thief of love, a crying form against the natural sea's wind

Inside the "hell chasm" you take apart your bones and put them
back together
Then you leave

It's very easy I've done it four times

I've spoken with SatanGod GodSatan in the leafy glade in Missouri

You might notice the building in which you sit is made up of light
You might notice that the words that you speak are uttered under
light
You might understand then that there is no place for god, the
cast-out

God is a runaway in a depression-era train
God is a paper-mâché sentence that you can throw away

Now, earth?

Or Streets or Smiles

I sat for a thousand years
Using smoke to measure time
If you don't look at the people, you'll know what I mean

Rather, a statue in likeness of a person precious and ancient
That awakened the memory of the flush naked earth
Exposed to the sunlight and made ancient
No, no you can't have it or go back

It's mine for just brief moments and I don't want you to see the
      corners of buildings
Or streets
Or smiles, because
I know it will make you sad

And the statue made all the difference in the wretched night
Because you know night makes the day often, and further,

It was ancient statues that made me look across a green morning
      lawn
A never seen way and call up from the ground

Water to drown the bliss and missed love notes scattered in the
      sunrise
Still ancient and permanent

A jungle lion keeps his hoard here and yes I can still hear you cry

Just the Same As You Don't Know

Pleasure walking in the smooth dark kitchen

Made wretched by a lack of good windows that would let the
  moon in

I washed dishes with you in a dormitory once and thought about
  marriage

And sometimes I wonder if it really was you

Beaten golden sun-days wring out the end of the moon by its cool
  sapphire shadow
That really was only a shadow, then and now just as it was before
  when I forgot to
Kiss you on top of the tower

But then you made food and loved an uncountable amount of
  other lovers, when
Someone told me that it was really true that you left a pattern on
  a cowboy's heart

I grieved for The Ramones and high school plays when you had
  forgotten about them
(my jacket smelling like stage makeup afterward)

Those images, like a white cat ancient on a moonlicked pavement
  staring, and then

Like a reverse charm, following me in the back of my SUV all the
    way along barren
Nebraskan
Highways

I of course went to all the places again, with a different intention,
    and dreams of others

But it really never is the same after the first time you leave for
    other skylines

It might have been you that made me draw a blood colored valen-
    tine while taking
Medicine that let in some black lightning demons to stab my back
    in my dreams

But I don't know

Just the same as you don't

Why are we both here, and then the sky turns dark and the moon
    comes out

The kitchen is somewhere in the future, because I would have
    never found it

Bereft of lightning and moonbeam and sacred trees and pictures
    of lost necklaces

And sometime I'll pick up a lamp and find that it wasn't a kitchen
    but rather the inside

Of some heart that was not a cowboy's heart but rather eucalyptus
    daydreams

Of a would-be modern vagabond

Shut the door.
It lets in ancient treasures, or rather lets them get out

Through the window.

Empty Blue Bed

If a tree falls in a forest, will anyone hear it
If a man cries alone, will anyone hear him

I saw a face today that made me suffer
I took it away with me, and now I wonder
How it can be that I have been left alone

Rhythms lose their sight when they are made
Because in their making is their end
Is their sorrowed lone end by which hearts are forgotten for other
    things

More exciting things, other beauties
That obscure the absolute Beauty

So that when looked at, when fathomed across long eras, only
    seem
Like breaths of a lover that doesn't exist

I knew that I had you then, flower of love
I knew I could pick you and cradle you and give you myself

But faces are just words, only more mysterious, only more
Only
More
Lost

And some sunrise will come again, I know, but today I cannot
      seem to breathe my faith
My faith in hearts that pass me by, and don't exist
Hearts that don't exist unless I make them exist, whereby
Destruction of happiness forms around an empty blue bed

In which I put down my search and give in to it

But I cannot give in now, I cannot go back
Go
Back
To the beginning page, the one there
That you just turned.

When the Sky Was Beautiful

But that sky is beautiful
The way the twilight dusts the air and leaves flecks of your memory

When you walked down to the ocean, before you saw it you
	remembered
As night rose over the hill
The way that you moved in the past, the way that sun killed the
	morning

Was like dusted black angels caressing pain

Ever you tell them again, ever you know
Ever you feel that swelling below
Ever the sea gives its new ancient happiness

You'll find the beginning of that dusk

I watched seventeen men with their pickaxes swinging
Destroy this building where I saw children who were seventeen
	chiding the world with
Broken glass

And they took the building down, they tore it down, a giant hole
	in the ground, now

Where you can see faceless memories

But nothing has been there since, and the deck of the ship where
you could have stood

Rolled away on that sea in your imagination, and the hill that

You climbed

Sang with the flecks of twilight

I tell you this now because
I tell you in rhythm because
I can't forsake what I'm telling you because

It's real

So take away your hats and shoes and everything you gave to him
when
You came home after you were married, and

Go beyond the sea and find that other hill exactly the same, ex-
cept descending and

Walk down it and see the town where you grew up and see every-
thing laid out

Before the rising sun

I know

That it will be there, if you only had stood

On that deck that one evening when the sky was beautiful.

Waves Are Like the Waves

You want to go to sleep but
You can't go to sleep because

Of a girl you met today from a far away island

And some other voice from the past is erased quickly before your
vision

And when you try to lie down and rest your head, you think

The joy of the island must be wonderful

Sometimes speaking you think of the sea
How it hangs down from the sky like a child's book
And the waves crashing are just whispers of a picture in the book
And the majesty of the unseen things is just another page
Because the world is getting smaller only in people's dreams
The world is getting smaller

Smaller

In people's dreams

And sailing down the pages you realize that it only grows smaller

For some

Because you know again how fleeting being a man or woman is
You know that having reached the top of some mountain, you can see

Below, that

Things you wished for are coming true, although you will never see them

And on the island, on that peak

Which are the same thing, you realize

That the world will never be small, and the gray sky of the waves are like the waves

You made when you loved, through which you can see many wonderful things

You will grow old with joy because what you have seen will always be new, if only

You can understand the way a door closes, and

How people love

Morning

10:30 train
With your bright fixtures and soft hands, you
Rumble and creak through the night like wisdom

And beside you lie dreams
Dreams sifting through the sand of darkness
Like melancholy waitresses
Bludgeoned by husbands, and cruelly
Thrown through edge-less doors

Swift and roaring, you parade
Through the forsaken lands and the heightened and dark sunsets
Over rivers that speak
With the fervor of millions of tiny chains, missing

But you ramble on, you old sire of the night
You old awakener of justice without meaning
For the dreams, they do not bleed you
They speak through the foggy night like you weren't there

How rudely you interrupt them! How plainly you see
That this coming of age for you was too late, this 10:32 PM

And you slide and rampage through the already sleeping faces of

Summer warmness, and

Everything seems all right to you, because every dream, every
  burdened shadow

You only touch for an instant, and then

Are

Away

To grapple mutely with the

Morning

Only seen through a mirror

Begin

I cleared down upon a moonlit beam
Wicked, washed and weary
From the ancient tide of seamless gleam
Wondrous, whispering weary

To where my father's keeper lay
Tormenting me to stay
Within my odious mind
Wicked, washed and weary

When sudden on that darkened bow
Come rain in cloud and thatch in brow
A woman spoke to me
The Sea.

In a whisper faint and low
She said, "Wait,
Goodbye Hello"
And all my sorrows grow
Tenfold on the snow

Lay me down, my weary box
Of pocketwatch and nick-nock
Of seamless tide and wretched hive
"Come with," she said, "to me."

So strangely have I waited
With warning breath bated
To the secrets unrelated
To this clock which Misers me.

And gentle as a wind
On diamond, crystal thin,
She said to me
"Wretched dog,"

      Begin.

Helmet

I grow weak
As I leech away
Each breath I speak
Against that love

I am against the fire
Of your graceful and warming touch
I take away all the things that you give to me

And I destroy them

Someone torment me for my time
So that I may live to be a gravestone

Someday

Why must the shadows that walk behind me
Describe me better than myself
Why must the anchors that bind me
Clutch wicked chattering lies

I am a weed
That grows to your feet
And begs for more
And I still speak
That I am joyous on my feet
When I leech

Your love

Remember that there used to be sacred children
That spoke as though they were in ideal happiness
On some mysterious and terrifying screen of helplessness

In America

I am not quite what you expected me to be
A simple wretch, and then women see

That I am nothing more than they want me to be
After they cleanse me and destroy what is mine

As I destroyed them

Begging to end a cycle, I put on a helmet

And dive into the rain

Please don't come back again.

Meadow

The things you make are equal to the things you break
Said the man through the mirror-shadow

And like the gripping hands of tomorrow

Made a way

In place of the window pane
She said again
In place of the way you made faces
In the quiet reading-lamp

Was enough to take my breath away
And go away to write some letters to the magistrate
Of police cars, of hidden bars

You've never been to

Place your hand flat against the pane
And with pain that strikes flurrying
Beauty it out

I lust for the meadow

Happen again, return
The wandering soul on the floor
And ragged wisdom churning
Before the door

I wished that I could have gone out of the
Long-lived and rusted chalices
That sat unused on the jewels of a far-flung land
Hidden forever

But you spoke and the pane was a-shattering
Beneath the horses clamoring
Before the door a-wandering

About your lived-long happiness

And the chains awoke me, rattling
The burning hatch of the bastard door
That evil smiling cruel beguiling

Meadow

Sick people only wash their hands
Before they make commands
And the linger of your breath on them
Makes them burn with madness

The licking of the pane is but an unnoticed gesture
Beside that old house on the meadow where you once wandered

As a boy

But when you were a small child your brain was not large, and
        you did not think
About the people in heaven and what they drink
About the missing way the people stayed

Before the house forgotten

They looked at you desperately, and with your hand you motioned

To it,

To them, but they were never there
Just sitting on the stairs
Before the wind took it away

And left you there

On the bare staircase

Forever, with the window in the wind.

Desperate Morning

Sitting between rainbows you spin, spin
Watching the last music as it begins, begins
There is another trickling going slow

There is a waiting for you now
There is a crumbling tumbling bow

In the night beside a plate with no food

I know there is a place which trembles greatly in the wake
Of only one piece of time which explodes without rhythm

There is nothing inside that jar sitting on the table

I bleed so slowly when you speak

Tomorrow, tomorrow, which day will their love grow
Which blind throe will ever know
How they pitch their tent so

I went downtown to ask a woman several questions which
She promptly replied that she had no food which to give

A loving throbbing father
In the cooling wishing winter of a day that
Spins downward like a dentist of the imagination

Eventually you may find something, but it won't be
What everyone tells you that it will be, and before
This night
Before
This day there will be some other kinds of people
Knocking at someone else's door and you will wish that

They had come for you, but they won't, there is

A droplet of whiskey soiling a glass that is placed before the
        ocean, just so
The ocean looks like it is in the glass

Sunlight beckoning down the sloping green hill flush with the
        trembling awareness
Of peace that only lasts for an instant before you realized that
        there are

People at home, people in your home
Places unknown that with singing twilight bemoan
A grand dry silence inside of another hall
That you wished forever that you could always recall
But heading due south in the desperate morning will only get you

Down the hill and a plate full of food and then you will

Forget in your other remembering.

Languid Night

My hopes
My dear
Tonight, I fear
Have washed away like forgotten leer
And left me here, in solace queer

Mirror of the languid night
With tree beams and leaden fog
That's creeping along the morbid bog
And leaving you, oh loving mob
Beneath my friendly foreign sobs
I trial on this languid night.

The croak, an ode
Of the mist below
The still sound
Of old hope

I feel, my love
If you were here
That this heavy night would have no fear

But you are not, and never will
Again aid me from damp'ning chill
Of April night, of sapped will
On this wondrous lip
Of wretched night.

So tomorrow I'll not pray
For you to come
Alight down on me from heaven rung

I see now that you're gone
Never under the same sea

Or dark, so sweet
This languid night.

The Scarlet Winding
Upward-moving Stair

There was a light in my driveway
On a December night so frequently miserable
That I took into my eye and cried
For the making of time

Whenever you see me
Walking alone
Whenever you see that
I'm chasing my home

Give me bread, and a place
To sleep so merrily
And without relief
From the rolls of your breath

Curtains of longing
Hold away your wiling gestures
And pin me to the sky
Against the February Vespers

And sing a song so endless in freedom
That it stops the rain and brings forth new jesters
And for a moment in watching repose
Does for the magic Satan re-close

Injure and malign this hard heart kind

And bring it down from the merriness found
Flock frothing frolic found frequently fair
And don't mock the scarlet, winding upward-moving stair

I don't want you to come back
No
I don't want that mansion in tow

Cry tears upon the wrinkling bed
Cry hope down from its heaven-bound tread

I saw a light in December so fair
I saw a light greedily take you by the hair

And mess you down until you were bruised and homeless
And flick you across the well-mowed ditch of

An original time, a lost bard's sweet reminder
Of gossiping skylines in city white paper
Of mingled obtuse and confused bits for later
That you gave up for the quiet of your paper savior

Shriek and moan against the sunlight
Which you follow so needlessly there
Bleed and groan for the dark light
Even mystery can lead you to home

But my home of the car lights
So mystically placed in the drive way

Is of my Love

Leaving

The House

Forever.

Wedding

You thought you knew what I thought
By what I said
You thought that you knew what I was thinking
Because you love me

But the sun doesn't part ways with the ground
And the mixed-in sound of the beating
Of the earth

Is true

Tomorrow plant a fountain of flowers that come out of the sounds

Mystic
The shore
Rhythm
Before

The crystal shimmer of dazes before the rhythm of mystic shores
Again

The light beside the fire, the one there with your hand on it
Is not for you, but rather is against everything that was believed
In the moment when you spoke the word, and then
Then
The company of them again
The chorus of a parted lip that gave itself to you in its fallacious
Words

And the tub where you put all the spare change from the wedding
Still sits there

Code in the meaning, and like a newspaper write on it with trem-
    bling hands as the
Story that was written crinkles without sound against your tear

Where have they gone?
Sweet Annabelle
Where have they gone today
Bring me a lock
Bring me a piece of your hair

So that I may tie ribbons down by the river and speak to myself
    about how
It was like when you were here

Yet the days, the days
Go by in a way
That puts it on a page
And forgets it

Because, because
The timing of love was
Beautiful yesterday.

Nightingale

Now among the frantic graces
You stop and admire the way the window moves light through
    the room
And everything breathes in silence

But there is something else you are missing
Something never around, fearing you

Treading beneath the waves

Gentle sprinkles of water kissed by sunlight glances
Divide you up into pieces
Which you see through the window

Before you lies the infinite space
The lighted and calling music of nightingales
That look down through you like tomorrow's promise

And everyone here at the meeting
Is so glad to see you, beckoning with your skillful hands
The moonlight shadow

However can you find it? However can you know
Between the mosses and the creatures that grow down below
However can you see it? However can it breathe

When it cures your every sickness with haunted mystery

Toiling forever the hoping eyes
Struggling against the crystal prism of the night
Which brings itself down so mesmerizingly
From the watchful flowing of the next day's sun

And the bliss that you return to yourself
Through a kiss through his mask
Haunts you like morning rooftops

Forever

Vanishes

It is quiet for some time, and you
Hear the wash of traffic like a distant rumbling of the past
And with the beginning of several voices, everything

Vanishes

But now in this moment, there is nothing beside you except
The reflections of your other days and it whispers like the

Dull and faded view of some empty court from a second story
    window

Where stone is perched and writhed with silent vines

And the sun is red, because you feel now that everything is in
    wealth

And the world is dying

It happened upon the warm snow
It happened on the folds below
It gave you a signal, like two eyes

In the dark, alone

And it told you, by and by
That what ever it is you tried to hide
Is like the red splintering of a still silent monster with big hands
Holding on to a broken heart

But the action leaves you, and you watch as the silence folds in
    around the courtyard
Pressing in and leaving flecks of sound like pieces of invisible
    confetti

That ring around the day

When this new breath of winter comes, this autumn will be
    folded in, too

A coat along your arms and a steaming cup of loneliness

Pensively the sun casts its seemingly immovable rays against the
    serenity of the moment

It is not as beautiful as you wish it to be, you say

As the courtyard fills in with snow outside your window

And you wish with some irritation that you had a fire in passing

But it is only a wish, and the night comes in its sacred way, never
    changing.

The Bed Is Made

I heard a story once
Where people could walk and say hello
Across the majesty of a thousand voices
Falling in love

But they cried out, No
They gave me something that I didn't want
They gave me a children's book
Of love

I fear for the wretch in a gutter
Who doesn't know that even though
There may be a hand for him

There may be a hand for him

He swallows hard, and drowns the gin
He takes it upon his withering chin
The gossip of the metronome

Of the thousand angels beating

Show me the way, please I beg you to do it

Show me the place, I feel as though you knew it

Show me the road, empty black and fluid

And bring a nocturnal cry of the ones who knew it

I should go now, it's getting late
Said a painter, with a face
That was lost in and out of space

I should go and make my bed

Sometimes rivers, by and by
They cry out, and drown you as you fly
Through a soaring wicked cry

For love, you see

But now how must I sleep? The bed is made
The truth is watching now in forgotten glade
Of the hoping that I'd hear you say

Don't do it
Don't do it

Goodnight, my sweet, good night my dear
Goodnight to those who forgot to hear
The plunging roiling whispering fear

Of never hearing those words so dear

Smile

You'll find that you can smile more often now
And the darkened strands along loosened hands
Bring you to the light

Before you begin the stations of love
Before you place it down
There is a ragged charm in the winking of the light
Across the way

That you see so emptied by
Every kind of person
Every kind of wish

Below

Grab and snarl and bite and lacerate
And in a moment of peace shoot them

Why? Oh why
Such words to split the sky
Trying again like a tyrant
To decide where the meaning lives

But you're smiling, now, you feel good
You feel like the beginning of a horizon-less waking
To a field of your past lovers
Who were not lovers, only thoughts then

But your eyes and your teeth
And your cheeks so fattened by the waves of life
That you wrinkle your face and smile, defiant
Of the oncoming second wave

And on the air
Take away those bloods you shed
And put them in a shed because
You loved it

Watch for the streaming light that is so obvious but is so
Wicked because you cannot

See it

And below your smile lie the deaf of heart
Lie the breaking songs
Like the chattering throng
Of the dead

But

Listen and learn
Beguile and be stern

Because in your smile returns

No chord, no blissful reign
Of the things that you could have done again
And all those violent things
Like the wishes you left singing

Beside a shed where you once put down some papers

Frolics like stone the images you once thought were like water

And cements them in an unexpected place, so when you return

And your smile is the answer, then you

Kill

All moments of peace

With peace itself

So that the violence is washed away and your living is the culmination

The very zenith of making it make sense again.

October Twelfth Two Thousand and Seventeen

I smoked a magic Korean cigarette and spoke to the devil
He stood on a ship and we talked as old friends, smoke issuing
    from beneath his hat

I went down to the grave where there was an intersection of my
    past and melancholy
Sweet in its remonstrance of the things that did me evil, and

The devil laughed and gave me a cup of coffee.

I watched tree beams interfold with the sacred sunlight of Earth,
    and thought about

How I was ready for love again

And how I would not allow some certain phrase or instance dis-
    turb me, much like

The way the seas were before god, or children of men and
    women, children of the

Mystery together

The earth is sexed with the decay of an odd spring in the midst of
    future failures of

Those that would betray.

I left on a balcony some wish for my favorite dream, and have
   never thought of it since,

Only to know that I became a man that day, so often frequently
   passed over in the night, this

Unholy botched place of mixed feelings and experience, and the
   intersection of the graves was

Alas poor god where I killed something inside me to allow for
   freedom,

And moving upwards into the ladder I fell down to the middle of
   the earth, and found it quite

Warm and pleasant, like a peasant fire hearth after a long day's
   travellings

And I finished my cup of coffee and looked at where the devil had
   been sitting, now gone, now

Moved back upwards somewhere, and from the center where all
   beauty was, I felt the similarity

Now it is gone, and cheap metaphysics litter the floor of the par-
   ish, unbound sheaves of papers
And
Letters, written with good intent but never bound and offered,
   just so they couldn't be

Burned as often.

Красота

Monsterheart

He cornered the light from yesterday and a deaf dead musician
    beseeched him
"Spake the dancer, go trod heavily on the graves of thine
    countrymen"

He stood in a shade, in the house where you can look out and see
    an endless glade

There you can become something you forgot to tell yourself yes-
    terday, you can decide once
Again

The l'esprit d'escalier

And in the room with the shade requires you to think on your
    feet without much knowledge of

How to go about reconciling your feelings with the hidden musi-
    cian, the hidden deaf
It was within your own home, you just didn't see it

And tonight there will be some slight minded visitors, those old
    blank inquisitors, checking

Up on you from your past, there will be an endless line waiting at
    your sleeping place.

I know it might not seem very elegant, but your window or door,
    perhaps your sitting room

Is just it: beauty, like the sea within a necklace, like the feeling of
    attachment or triviality resting
Coquettishly against the shadow of what is beautiful about going
    abroad and singing to yourself

In the midnight time, in the broken time, in the waterfall of
    memory, or pasted on rose petals

I saw you in a garden, unapproachable, it was night and there
    were roses

And I devised an elaborate plan to seem somehow attractive or
    otherwise endearing, when all I

Could say or tell you about was my monsterheart

I don't write very often about it, so sometimes it is some pain to
    keep it within a jar on

Top

Of

A dying wish of a dying fall of a sunset which you did not see,
    and you saw the vision,

The corpus leaning like a firefly midnight dream on the end of a
    moon petal, and whispering

About pirates and the sun, she left out, she rescinded, and tragi-
    cally, somehow, the day came

The day came, O day

What will I do with my shadows now?

But the music was stuck on, and the ghost of Beethoven crinkled
    up sunlight on the far forest

He only made through music, and you felt you liked ghosts, be-
    cause they could only be seen

In morning, in death, in light and pain and you wished quietly
    again for the velvet marrow of

A tomb for your memories, then that's when you knew when you
    were in love and you

Remember what you wanted to say yesterday

Worth It

The moonlight touched a tincture of tobacco and said goodbye

I couldn't remember but you did, and I thanked you because
there are a thousand

Ways to be alone

I want to make the most of my time, I thought I heard her say
Giving way
To just what it was that was left on a doorstep last summer

But making the most of your time is not something you wear,
something you buy,

Something you place in a window on a forgotten day, but it is
blue tinged photographs from
1993, sweat-stained baseball gloves, love of what was beautiful in
a small innocent town

Love of what was gracious enough to keep your heart, a piece of
it, and what really
Was
Worth it, was just as you were, with your black hair and stories
about spiders and witches

Stories about punk and I can't help myself, anymore

I can't let myself see you unless you'll grasp at my love, so absent
    and forgotten
So latent in the midwinter, I'll try to make myself worthwhile, I
    think

She said.

But these words she will not know, she will not understand unless
    they are delivered
By
The crystalline postal man of the morning, in the cocoon of peace
    shrouding from wickedness

In short, I will appear in a photograph from 1993, and I will try
    to speak about just how much

I loved her

Yet she won't know, and all those struggling days of late child-
    hood, watching the end of the ship
Go down, down into the wreckage of bliss, I might know just how
    many crows woke me

Prayed for me their cackling song, that one gray morning in
    March at the old house, a house now

After and again

Filled with memories, don't visit there, this, here, is where you
    cried, this is where you

Made love this is where you decided to leave and this is where the
    aliens festered and made
Illusions in the midnight dust, made cries of shrill silence against
    my wishing

And here, in its preciousness, is where I learned how to play guitar, and it is in blue photographs

And matching laughs and eloquent timeless spaces where I play hide and seek with my future

My beloved one.

Bach CD on Repeat

The longest poem ever written
Was never written

Hold Your Gun

To drink in the first soliloquy of life
You must first walk down unpaved roads
He was nothing but an American pirate

The skill with which he once spoke to women, seemed
Valiant in lightness
To die

I remember, he said to himself one midsummer's afternoon
What it would have been like had that door there been cast in a
    different light

But as it stands, there are only certain things you can see certain
    ways
At certain hours

Because of your choices, he said to me.

Standing in line.

Punctuating the rainy night with the drive through the empty
    parking lot
Were silver ghastly premonitions that gave birth to sucking sorrow

The marrow of the night seeming to dry up, withered in the place
    where he drove the car
Where others would be tomorrow, they seemed to bleed him out

I can't, I won't go back
I don't wish to, I don't want to hold your gun
I do, I do love you
Blinking in a goldenrod meadow in the sun

The door was quiet, and slanted in the midafternoon way
And I know those trees, evergreen seams, would have been
    enough to put your dreams away

Minnesota in the night

I wished the villains would have kept at their game, and kept
    playing, instead of them giving way
To the rusted dust of death, which wasn't so black, wasn't so un-
    pleasant, just a faded windowsill
Memory

But as it stands now the villains are dead, the parachute woman
    grieves in part, and, however

Dead

They still sing their song

It was odd to see the prostitute sad beneath the glowing green
    amber-light of the night king club

The king of clubs, me and the must of spell-books, keeping com-
    pany in the lurch

I dream, I seem, it goes, it goes
And when you lost it that's when you knew what it was

Good-bye, I wanted to say, he said.

Good-bye.

Punctual mornings are difficult for the debauched man, who
knows how to sew rainbows in

The queen of hearts

Sky-borne meadowlark

Which is where I would have proposed to you, on the dirty happy
farmground

She was nothing but an American pirate, in likeness of the
twisted flesh of love

Groaning Midnight Black

What's your favorite thing to do? Do you like to do it alone?

Whence upon the summer grass is the truest beauty shown
When tomorrow is simply but an evening's last caress

On the rummaging confused and humble distress

What's your favorite thing to do? Do you look up from a book
And notice that time's gone by and not forgiven you your take

Not lingered in or whispered on about the morning you might
    not see
Not crippled sin or laughing when you dropped the pearl of wishes

And thanking him and a goodnight kiss and the rain against the
    shadow
And moving then, and wishing when you wake upon the morrow
    that

Someone had left you an obscure note that rang with the silence
    of the approaching dusk
That rang that sang that broke your heart which crumbled into dust

I know that you went to that cavernous memory-hall
Where when you were a child you stopped to stumble and fall
When you were in love you walked hand in hand with the one
    who was your all

And now I know and now I see that you someday would be alone
It is in the receding of the morning that you remember just as well

The columns fake and the hall you made around the beauty of it all

And when you told me and when you broke along the groaning
       black
The misfit tithe the wrangled mind the groaning midnight black

I developed an insignia for such times long ago when I was born
It didn't have to happen that way, it didn't fill you with scorn

I just lost it when I fell in love, that's all; lost it in the sea
Don't bother me with what you're free of, just listen once to me

Now I can't remember how many times that hall, with a slant of
       light from within
A fantasy of a still chamber of ruins atop a hill beneath the sea

What kind of light moves through water? What is the name you
       give to misery

Growing tired, growing weak, I splinter in the evening-time I lose
       what began to make
Me cry I lose

Those ends of something
What is your favorite thing to do? Do you like to do it alone
When the dreams against the silent screens break evenly for you

When laughing in the darkness you come up with a plan

For those images burning white on a beauty

The summer shade grins full-bodied and free of pregnancy, run-
       ning free

And going down among the sound of cheerful mockery there's

A place you say and go on without pausing over coffee
The rain dripping filled with your wishes off the balcony

Going home is not as hard as being free

Virgin Paper

I seem through a crack in your laugh
To carry what you want
I seem, I seem, you say

To love you

But I look backwards and along the field of time, there are mil-
    lions of hearts

To understand how to start, you have to start from the start
I think she said

Chasms charm you and the fear of the thousandth star drives you
    away
Drives you down and from the form you created this lust
This insatiable coinage of phraseology and bullshit sciences that
    make
Men into pseudomen

Yet I seem through a part of your smile
To want whatever it is you give me, in blazing confused chapters
Of seamless love in drowning past walking through topaz places
    you
My sweetheart dear you my love why is it that your name . . .

She screamed something and you didn't hear, turning down the
    death-lane with a turned
Collar and invisible black cape which you drew over the shad-
    owed street and made the
Scream into a carving, a wrong and seemingly endless belonging
    which you then

Wrote

I play matches with the deathlane Cindy Con capsule-woman
Who told me to come back home and say I love you

But none of these things are as important as what it was I forgot
    to tell you

Except if I forgot to tell you, then somewhere you left your gloves
    and I fetched them
Saying "I will marry this woman"

And the words of it became patterns in the street, and the black
    marks on the untainted
Virgin paper

Might as well not have been written at all if that woman had said
    the same thing, but

She didn't say the same thing and you know she never had it in
    her and so then
Candles must be blown out on the wreaths of midnight sadness,
    the dramatic other
Gladness which you
Like a laughing coffin took to the empty suburban street with and
    talked to the devil

Have not you heard
Have not you felt it
The shaking of the limb
The talking velvet

Sheets, they say, flail in the wind because

And only if

You let them

Worship-places

Solemnity in the white church
Blood shows best on white

You can only dream it if you are dead

It will be in the clean, sanctified, righteous and calm places of the
    caverns of
Humanity

That chaos will be most present

It is on the snow-white, cloud bosom of the world that death
    erupts most
Plainly

It will be upon the quiet hillside graced with the poison of god
    that one will see clearly
How fake it was.

Chill for me a glass of the wine of sin
I grieve when they called me that

I grieve when what is most good and holy in this world is di-
    gested through the spoken
Word
In

Worship-places talking about the past

God is not in the past but in the future

I dreamed again about you, about a screen with locks and fixtures
About a green screen upon a hillside viewed from within a magi-
cian's cataclysm

From within a house against the ire

Come speak with me against the holy people, come lie naked in
the soft letting, the
Dream space in the cool summer twilight with a half-worn blan-
ket, shining eyes and

A rich glade filled with the muttering of night

Come speak to me in a quiet winter room with open shades and
gently throated scarves

Come speak to me among the violets

It is comfortable in the non-god secret of the world because the
stars have no maps, the

Countries

Have no lines and the world is grinning in its body, not because
of it but because
Those clouds are not heaven, they are imagine

Curl into the sound of the river as the night becomes potent and
forget believing

The hillside will still be there when you awaken.

Coupon for the Dead

That selfsame night
Stood brooding by the waking light
The painted page of remembrance

The ending rhythm of what you were
Against the flowing pastures
Victuals for the mourning

I came here to see you, standing alone
I came through the window in a loan
I paid my way through heavy skies

I paid my way through the rain

Wait, said the selfsame speaker
I come wintering for you

Come with me, nighttime faker
You'll drill in the forgotten bliss

I do not know how heavily this night sleeps with thee

The rotten gut of the forest with the dead trees growing out of
    graves, and I opened up

I shut the door and dove into the nothing of where you used to
    find me

I grew a planted field of the wretched designated names which
    bind me

I in the selfsame night haunted miraculous exorcisms of a cup of
    coffee

With friends which betrayed me, and then spoke directly to the
    ground

I needed again in the night that rhythmic killing which founded
    me

Greedily I spoke to the winter and gave it penance
Greedily I designed what took me, and then through the sound

Through the going down, I charted against the flamboyant sub-
    way rail the crossing of the end

It doesn't matter, said he wailing, said he waiting for the phone

It doesn't matter, she said patient, she said wrecked without a
    home or a chance to find

That payphone that reaches into none other than that speaking
    place, that masked face

I gave straight to hell, and
Nothing you said can divert my wishes of conquering the dust

Nothing said can make it so I dream To-Go Coupon for the dead

Anyway

The lamps cooled and night brought forth its moon-ray
I sat in the glade where the hot day cooled around me like peace-
    ful ghosts

Don't take out my heart unless you want it

Some forests remind me of where I could have been had I not
    tried so much

Dried amphitheaters stuck in deserts become a new religion hot
    in the west, and
The succor of blind palms transpires against the dream-ridden
    night, which really was

Just like the day only fifteen miles away

In between the woes and the trifles and the calm roaring troubles
    which you wrote down, today
Are just chieftains of what beauty lies in the sand

There is nothing in that religious desert because the wind in
    secret times like now blows down
From hell or heaven, and coils away all the lines drawn there

It is a secret time but not a secret place, your feelings and in some
    birthed moment you'll
Understand that the time was kept on a New Orleans drum

Across those fifteen miles lies a bandit gang thrifting for the true
    hearts which are too hefty
And carry with them too many merits to fit in just one suitcase

Anyway

Closing swiftly across the many miles between here and the deaf
    light of night is only
What you wished for, not what they said or not what they put in
    your mouth or not what

Is lost so elegantly and spitefully through the bars and chains of
    conversation

It was just that, your eyes when you did not speak, that I couldn't
    throw out into that desert

And the bible of the myth is the light quick footed wind which
    you know contains
An endless
Drove
Of knowledge

But tomorrow when you find out what kind of secret times are on
    that drum, remember that
It's beating was just the same way that the world was before light,
    and night breathlessly

Incorporates the fifteen miles it took for you to be among the stars

If only the right angle could be achieved, but you don't know
    where to walk and neither do I

So if we are left wondering which way to go, can't the sound of
    the moon-ray bring it?

Cannot you feel

New York

It's not the only place where beggars and fools chide the darkness
It's not the only place where king comes on gilded shore
It's not the only place where love conquers madness
It's not the only place to be alive

The Priest Smoking

What happens in your home, because

That was the summer I got happy

What happens in your home, behind cool sheathed doors, cool
    sheathed rooms
Kept silent away from the invasion noise of fools and kept
    countrymen
What keeps them away you know quite not, you don't understand

Their rescinding, except in a tall wine glass filled with water so
    silent in a halflight
So brilliant in an eye, which sees it from behind where you stood
    and remains fixed

Where you stood a moment ago, not more

Jesters of the new kingdom wear the clothes of the old
High leaping racketeers of history, so we're told
They teach you the same things, and they listen to the noise and
    repeat it

Like a manmachine with fingernails for vinyl music grooves, like
    preachers with
Sullen sedentary moods, like preachers who smoke

The priest smoked in the door whenever you didn't look and
    something told you
He was wrong about something he tried to tell you once when he
    came to your house

I feel like there's a mystery in and within those ancient clocks, the
    ones that have kept time
From before you were born, but I don't care about them

Let them be flung into the recesses of the universe and take this
    walk with me

Come see the beauty inherent, why, I can't tell you, I can't answer
    questions now

I left the answers foundering at my other door

The glass was picked up and another day's light shone on the
    empty table, and you were there
You saw me, I know you did, and because you saw me you were
    in despair and I

Not so secretly, now

Was glad of it
Charms the eastern sun, kingdom come in the mail

Sing the ache and dismiss it, you'll know if Keith wants you to
    play, anyway, he said, seeming to

Wink, but

Losing touch with the horizon, instead feeling like sunlight wink-
    ing through a sea's lost willows

I know the color is blue, today, and it is my happy strength in the
wake of pains through which

I accept and shrine only the bad day cleft-hangered red views of
water, because above the fire

Place

Of your death mansion I see a clear blue day with a painted sun
and joys from various travels

Such as a finely ornate elephant coffin made from blackened
bone, and cheerfully I

Quote from a scream and give to my dream it's love

Gruesome, you looked on in all your lonesome glory

Waves of the Noon

Now the noon has quieted,

I see a part of the horizon missing
The other life to which I cling

A life emblazoned with joy and children,

The children I might never have and under a cloak of night
The noon is forgotten

Why is it that you go down there, to that grove where you cannot
  see the horizon?

Why do you place it in front of me like an iron-clad edifice of a
  car from the '30s,

Why does then become your question, it rests like cheap lips in
  the second-story bathroom,

Rests like cheap ships crashing against a black flag woman

Do they come together? Do they ask?

Inside the brilliant grove is then a sculpture which cries, and then
  when you lift it up, it matches

As perfectly as wretched hearts can, the bliss of the missed horizon
The horizon that you didn't see was all around you, and all
    around the town, the glass dancer

Chieftain dancers with their spreads of eagle wings and their clay
    and blood, stifled by the
Concrete that once swept away their lives like the way the cloak
    now sweeps away those
Gluttons at the table of mercy,

I know you do not send Cupid's spear in a vain way, trellising
    macabre victory light broken
By the waves of the noon

Because it was in a perfect noon where the horizon became what
    I missed in love, what I
Carried aghast in the presence of women on women, once, when
    I didn't quite understand

And now papers from two-story chambers speak of liquid gem
    sitting places and smoke
Rotted out unto the ceiling, not blown about by an annoying
    wind, not taken out and set
In life, but comfortable in death, because yesterday

Is dead

And if you didn't know it look at yesterday's horizon—the part
    you didn't see
Crouching sinister and looking at you from a crow's peak, the
    back of the top of your hair

Which is why you wanted to know if your other life bore children
    because they don't bear
Children now and there's something sinister
Just because you can't look there doesn't mean that you can't
    know, and softened expensive
Lips don't kiss you or take you but issue forth sounds, grinding
    the merciful into the ground

And telling you that it wasn't too sensitive to ask about your story
    that night, rather

A drunk's lip dispatching police orders and the simple formation
    of the word "begotten"
In an outside of church conversation, and that's when you knew
    you were alive

Again or perhaps at the first

True Ones

Maybe the most powerful ones were black

Not like some white ones, that cut with truths like Merlin's sword
    dipped in winter

But with a surge and an onslaught of power, merciless healers
From the black well of humanity.

They come to me now, in my most sane and insane times
Telling me to move this way or that

And in my most fragile times, with the choice of seeped laugh
Echoing through otherwise doubted weak chamber, echoing

Or not some men, white

Who circumscribe their own kingdom with the voices so bluely
    cruel in the moonlight
They make weeping, but

Perhaps they were black, the truest ones

Because they already know and go further, beyond into the fron-
    tiers of humans or suffering
Which are the same

Strong handsome, wise with bones, both of animal and ancestor
Rummaging through what the others did not dare to look at,

And to borrow nothing and lend sparingly so that the rest in
        America the Americans might
Tell

Strong handsome gentle with souls, because they know them and
        cut them down daily
And with music

And if they are weak, white one, they are weak because of you

And no other

And maybe they were the most powerful.

Walking Path for Nigh Hearts

But I have no lover
The blossoming firs

I left it behind where you could still see the burn
I left it, I kept it instead in a package for the sacristy

I wept for a long year, I cherished how deeply they feared I would
go away

There is nothing left for you here in this old house except the
gemstones you laid
With bare hands and bare back against my thistle body, the
combs of the shore
I went away, way down where the was no light any more and now I

Stand

Helpless and free, at the bottom of the tunnel I saw for so long, so
many grievances

Went out of me, so many believing friends that I now know noth-
ing of

You're gone, now, forever, free, listening, cherished, blistering deep
The past of myself, and I know that in some time there may be
other pasts of myself

My fingers tremble at the cup, I can't go so far as I used to be able
    to go

The edge of the universe still moves out away, and some kindly
    say, they go to stay

When they leave me lurched in the Midwestern sun, which they
    never took the time
To understand

The house gradually empties, the ghosts and the gentries, the same

I placed my hand down in the running rainwater down on the
    street and exchanged souls
For turquoise and shoals where I can oft keep what I came there for

Now my gods are music and beneath this rock and roll are the
    end leaves of it,
Now my gods are Sitting Bull and Standing Bear and Geronimo
    and love, it breathes

Like a swaying sigh and you knew that Nebraskan sunset was
    really Sioux

Lakota, and now I've said too much and need to

Go outside or build a door at the bottom of the stairs or tell you
    nothing more,

Said it, said she, said me.

My Number

While I'm in my car I might as well drive to paradise
Said the sometime contortionist, perhaps homeless

Man

I leapt into the visage of the sun yesterday, sometimes wondering
    where all the
Vaporized pot hole dreams go

You can look under the rock beneath the stream, but you can
    stand against the rocky bank
Of your childhood and look in and see it, and like a lost piece of
    furniture wander into

The bookstore and have a subtle pained flirtation with the pale
    eyed book associate

Who knew that you were single but you don't know, love

You don't know dear you don't know darling how much I care,
    like a flock of sometime
Part-time
Spellmakers the sunshine comes looking for me, and what was
    most charming about you

Was the way you noticed the spider beside your sunshine Portu-
    gal friend

I know how many times you've seen the death of hopes by the
     way you associate your eyes
With unyielding romance, and what you cover up

What you don't understand is how to achieve a sleeping-place of
     comfort and wealth

Make up your own wealth because baby it's not going to happen
     otherwise

I sat brooding over life in the psychiatric hospital on the girls'
     side while the boys drew knives
And yelled, and all they could do was in secret tell me I was play-
     ing it

We watched *Fat Albert* and *Legally Blonde* in the hospital and the
     rain came down in the middle
Of the room, and a thousand other things happened like the rav-
     enette girl who might still have

My number

But sometimes I wonder

If you still understood all this, because your eyes were watching
     for the sweet removal of despair

I don't know if I love you because I don't know if I love myself, yet
     until I do

Tell me what kind of books you write, and I'll sometime in the
     gleaming hour of crisis

Chant them and sway them down through the rain and the con-
     tortions of paradise, while at once

Pining like Christ beneath the evergreens of my child's memory,
my childhood home, and then

Sometime in September leave myself in the dust

Can I Fix You

By the light you lay out your clothes
You set out your clothes for revolution

By the dark you see the same throne
The seeds that were sewn for your returning

I know how many times you went down by the road
The end of the road of your hometown

I know by the shards of your broken up heart
That show up stranded in your shieldless face, that

You knew just how to break them

But don't worry, don't be sad at the turning again of the stop light

Don't be worried about the return of glory to the one thing that
    you missed

The road that ran by your wholesome home town came grieving
    through a Scandinavian
Subway

And the place where you put down your pieces of heart became
    again like a road-way

It crashed through the forest, it made a loud sound against the
    backdrop of your calamity
It rustled and prayed it rushed and gave way for the building of
    what you were here for

Violent shades of a mirror that once hung in the teenage room,
    with lipstick drawings and
Kisses of dawning and the one left shoe that you put on the tree
    by the bridge in the city

That you had written "Can I fix you?" on

I know that this mirror that once swooned by the bedside became
    like fire and shattered
It splintered into a broken heart and the only one that could get it
    back was the rose grower

The gardener of shadow and the masked knower

The syndicated beauty of thought flying like rain against the
    flower-like blooming of
The cracking open of heaven and each color becoming like a feel-
    ing enough and for long enough

To become a person

To become just how and with each grave bow the strings of your
    home-road dispersed, here.

I know where they went, I know how they sent you
That is why you must bow to revolution
The actualization of what heart you left on that road with
With specific pink smiling and a natural beguiling
Of the beauty of loving in sin

You speak to me plainly and yet I still fail to see

The inward workings of dawning as you strike heavenward with
the old highway covered
In twilight and through the smooth windshield the dirt and dust
smoothing out the pathway
Two thousand revolutions per minute as you level out on that
cracked cement stairway

Somehow

In Order to be Significant

I crept into a crypt
That was sweetened with your imagination

I gave up on the winter side
Of going together with someone lovely
I left it, sodden and bereft
In a grave-place naked in the swiftly, sodden sun

Do not wonder how I got to this place
Said the man holding the torch
It was in the middle of the street where I buried my dreams

Do not ask me how I got here, said the doorman
Rightfully wandering across the in-between space of what I had
    made for a grave

What I had loosed in the night, what I had planned for your flight
Above waves

And a coarse ringing, disrupting heavenly bodies because
None

None

There's something else I forgot to tell you about the crypt

Grinning sun-days are the same as doorman nights, wet and
    cold-dripping
Festering and street lamp hiding

The chider that entered through the mark made by cars

I grow sad in the expression of your eyes
I grow with each momentary silence, the silence that comes from
    speaking

The end of the beginning of ideas and the vomiting of the rest of
    them
And it smelled like swill, a wretched-up breath of alcoholic

And somewhere in the middle of the road there were plans made,
    and I left through a
Future

I don't know where you put it, I only know where it grew from

In the crypt is the head of the one you loved
Because it needs to happen swiftly in order to be significant

Grapple with the end of the beginning of thought, and think of it
    instead
As being saved for cherished eye-gleams on a forgotten shore

That was clearly in the place where I went
A house alone by the shore within the middle of the street

That I left with you, instead greedily taking up a head from a crypt

And crying about how when I'm ghosting it will never be alike

Written Alone

Another autumn another chain of memories
Another autumn another stillness in the sea

Let it go

My friend, to the shadow which you know
Let it go my friend to the sea

You were in time with the autumn sunlight girl
But now in the stillness moved about the world

You see her go
And what you know is that what made you show to her
In time
That sea

Which if you can find the timing in your mind then the end, my
    friend

Is how you came to be

Just what it was and quarreling because you let it
Not from an argument with the sky but from the smelting of a
    heart

Which tore you apart and said look down

Look down the rotten pale ground and

Besmirch the things you see, those climbing memories and

Kill them with the sun

Because at the end of that sea, those rotten things are

Not to be found because what it was you found was not a song in
the sea but
Rather what made the sea, and being from the grounded families
of the dusk

Being from the founded families of hearts you knew that when
you were left apart

You couldn't see just what it was, but along the ground, looking
down, down

Was the end of the memory as it was

Evangeline

We watched a pirated copy of *Paris, Texas*
On a moon divided by the whispering plain
In between secrets, sacristies, endings of things

I felt you in the distance
And on that road I made them listen
Made them in time like stone

Evangeline, Evangeline
Broken tithe and harangued dream
I listened through the doorway
Of the heart of the moon
Inside the ends of the pickup truck gangplank songs

Then, like crows, you approached with the rain
Chiseling mountain living, pious and incomplete
Your heart a robe of sacrilege

To hang mysterious pictures of them on

And you fought in the war and you made the end climax and you
    discovered gold what
Sounds do they make in their half-death sleep?

Sounds of empty parking lots beside buildings built in the

Post-1989 children's fair the
Tips of racketeers and gun-shy Moliere blanking the sky-cathe-
dral persons in the pictures

And like a profane relic the man-slave of Evangeline declared
bankruptcy

And fixated star falls, watery star-fellings

Manic Church

You spent time thinking about how they could die

How they could, in time, be like it
But you found out how they've decided
To go on without you

There's something they wanted to tell you and I'm here to say
what it is

Growing patterns of lives against the backdrop of the corporation
wall
Cease the strumming of the blasphemy girls that you always, you
always

Take with you even though they miss you when you're with them

Some kind of blasphemy girl, you say, turns out to be just what
you wanted on that
Beach in the sunset where you killed the guns-for-hire the high
schoolers

Who wear those certain faces at truth because they can't see it

There was a person who dropped their lines successfully and had
        such a good time
With the married girl, until the blasphemers had their head for it

This is what they wanted to say:

Someday the earth will eat up walls and find out who made them
        but in the meantime
Fix a meal and brew some strong drinks and have your enemies
        to a party

Where you can feed them delicious secrets about what they
        wanted to say

Because, hand in mouth, they will chalk you
They well will walk upon you
On your birth day

There is only one time for you to be having it, and it's in this time
        when there are another thousand voices that you wish you
        could save and say to them what it was you wanted to say
        but there is a blessing being said in another manic church
        the religions of the birth and when they're done walking a
        musician will spit in your path and you'll see on top of the
        buildings just how far it will take for the moss to grow on
        them breathe what you feel sometimes is a mistake upon the
        sodden ground and like a sound begin to say

What you want to say

They said this:

We build a church of bliss
Where you can kiss your dying day and make some sort of brew
        and all those other things

Because the smell of chalk is what gave you away

Entering through the back door is the ghost of your love, and
    inside your lover
Is the fungus that sunlight makes on your breath invisible

And emanating from the specter is the reason that they did die,
    those blasphemes

Woe

The cruel hospitality of the drunk to the sober
In the battles on the front lines of infamy

I saw it shaped in the graying beard of a so-called expert
Flying away from him as though he intended to give off the feel-
    ing that it was

Too dark to see

And somewhere in between these lost and crying days
Is a shard of frozen maligning of what is really there behind those
    skeleton faces

It seems as though
What you wanted to know
Is lying dead in the sky
Is breathing

But I know, when you find it
The things that remind it
Will lay it down smoothly
In the sunset

Because you can't come along to the place where these people
    who were at the bar
Are really shown and fooled into themselves, like a painter in a
    mirror of a painted

Skeleton face

Then sometimes you'll know how finally to grow cold in the summer time

I needed to show how seventeen is death, here

And everyone that watches you and doesn't talk to you does more to you than
The people who talk to you, because they don't understand
How deep the sadness in themselves is until they see
Like a painting
Their own faces in the mirror put up for them with words, and they don't understand
They
Don't
Understand
How difficult it is to really be happy
And how difficult, my love, it is, to find you

Sometimes the so-called expert with thousands of children bell-choirs from churches

Comes down around my dreaming place and clangs them so that the music I once
The music I once heard is

By far

Against me

Until I have to rip up sofas with knives and declare a state of independence

From myself, I don't know how

These wars that go down and chalk up to infamy
Are really just marriages

And the beginnings of marriages, and

Everything you loved can still be there after some time of grief
Woe woe woe woe

Inclined toward the sloping dream, you

Are embarrassed to see your naked soul, when it was only

The sides of where you put your coffee cup and you awakened

Flailing madly into the dawning sun
Like someone who is acting tries to do

Each time you can't miss, even though you wanted to.

In a Different Way

You cling to the planet
Its surface, so thin and covered with whispering seas which you
    could never
Cross, because you didn't have time to do it

Then you walk, the leaves making small sounds beneath your
    feet, and you await
The snow

Which will come tomorrow, if not for the beginning of today you
    would wonder about

How everything would go up into the sky

Some strange thing keeps your feet locked to the ground and you
    smell the air filled
With early signs of snow, and the diamond-cities bristle upward
    and cut the sky

How could you leave me, my love
How could you go away
When the night is near me, my love
With your embrace so far away

The surface on which you walk and the things which extend
    upwards hopelessly into
The sky
Will be soon covered with the silk-sound of light coming from
    the past
And you wonder how your feet will not leave the ground

These places that you loved and loved in, these movements on the
    earth
The heightening fear of tomorrow
Come between us, my love, and bring us sorrow

In beside the bed where you put a candle-light
Lies no picture of the past, because when you were out walking
    today and you felt
The ground beneath your shoes and the leaves which made little
    sound, you thought

About a day covered in the feelings of the future, which now, with
    time, has arrived

In a different way

Charms cover the wrists of the sea which holds itself around the
    bristling skylines of
The attempts to block out the sun and live forever in buildings

I know that when you cling to the planet it suffers, just because
    everyone

Must cling to it and then go be down in it, someday

And someday, my love, comes sooner than tomorrow, because
    the sky, and the past
Unite as one in that scraping, covering day when you lie lifeless

But

Tomorrow is not today, and while the sun rescinds quickly

Cling, cling to the ground, and remember that your feet held there

By galaxy-exploding gravity

Is not a coincidence, but rather, in time, by your bedside

Makes you into who you are, and you won't leave

Here

Until you close your eyes and miss it and are left in the cold blue dark

Of the rest of the universe, in which

No diamond-city can be found, and where you will never be.

Old House

It was easy to make the day a memory
Because the day gave itself to you, what did you think

When it gave itself to you

Sometimes you go around that old place, that whispering old
    house
Where you died
Where you put flowers on yourself

And you think that it was the beginning of something

Wretchedness in dreams, they make you who you are
You think sometimes, and see

How it paves a way

The belief that you held tonight was again like always

Some cheered and well-spoken door

And where you died, the place that I'm telling you about
The place that right now I'm telling you about

Was in the future, was in your dreaming

Because now is the day when you make it, now is the day
The very same day

When you begin to care, because

Your dreams are different entirely from your house
Where

On a solemn day

You became like death in your hopelessness

Yet this very place that I'm telling you about is your love

Brought with joy like wreaths of sunlight in the middle of the sea

Deep in

Without a care, like freedom

Was the night, when the old house

Creaking in your dream, became

My friend

Like the water falling down from the trees after the rain came
     around you

And told you what it was like

To live.

The Autumn of Your Heart

In the autumn of your heart
I spell a word, a song, a binding
That brings you to a knee

In the middle of the spring

It was a cold gray garden where the bells came down
It was a naked garden, a place where you put some kind of

Song for the end

But I don't want you to leave, I don't want to see it come down
    again
I don't want it to breathe down my neck

Some other time you wished for the radiant conundrum
Which began in you

But fading is the face which made you in your place
Precious is its leaving
The loving hope of tired eyes

Which brought you along to a place where you couldn't sleep

It was in the designations of some deities which threw you
    around, around

Threw you around in them for a while, threw you placidly onto
the sun-wetted concrete

Where you dried up and spat with vehemence that you thought
you had left behind

But naked in the gray garden you hear the tolling
And forgiving you is the place which made another face you
wished for, tired, eyes not moving

In the autumn of your heart

And again something chides you, makes you suffer
When you thought the sea was more than just a wasteland of love

When you thought that face, as you clothe yourself in the garden
and it springs to color

Was the very twilight of your beating breast against the swelling
of the downturned way

The highway

From your love

Children of the Sky

If I could say
Some word or diamond from my mouth
Some trifling thing that throws down its weight through you like
    sand

Then I would give it to you

But time is cruel
There is a painting, somewhere, that will wither away

There is a painting of me

But there is also another place for you to find me

It is in the breath of the rain, it is in the washing of the earth

Made clean by a cloaked and masked grotesque thing

Only able to come out in words, in pictures

But most of all, in you

I don't forgive myself for anything I have done
I do not write my heart onto pieces of paper because

Someone will one day take this piece of paper and throw it into
    some garbage

And I will be hurt like a poisonous, stinging monster

But some things, like the way a star moves when it feels it needs
to

Or the way children of the sky perch loving hands upon their
mother

That I turn my head, for once, and see that beauty

In a glass eye, so fleeting but so real, so mysteriously gone

And some power leaves me when I see

Stars lose their meaning.

A Piece of Open Doorways

Can you walk down
Onto the golden ground
And make a sound
Which cannot be found

I want to know where you have received
Your trifling burning disease
Which you bring down for the eternal sound

Of the quiet frustration of inaction

I wish to make for you
Everything that you do not want
Because I understand it to mean

Your life.

I do not ever want you to come back
Here
There is something about the way that you cling
So frequently to my mind
That ruins it

Go now to your city
And bring me what you left there
A piece of open doorways
And nothingness

Alee

Tonight let music, let some sound
That you heard before on a rainy day
Come with you and show you how it is
Come with you to this night of power and protect you

I went across the ocean on a memory
Finding the ship out of the sky
Looking backward across the foundry
Of a million looking tides
And cried out like the blossoming of the bygone power of true
    speaking

Which found you along the shore

And with the hurting glances you showed the fever
Strike down the noise of the other sound
Which comes like silence through the wall and binds your hope
    from wishing

The beginning of the night is the signal of everything
If only you knew what to say
But tomorrow is today
In that old sacred way

Bring the torches of remembering

And inscribe it on the brows of those sweating angels that cruelly
   called you home

In the other morning

Because when you make your own designations on the brows of
   ships

Then the music will begin without stopping

And the wonder that you feel, you felt you could feel, tonight
      beneath the Milky Way
Destroy every wonderful piece of sunlight for it pales with this
   understanding of death

That you feel in you

Begin again what you started, because it was always the same
      thing
Trove through the field with a plow of joy
The end of returning is the quiet truth making
So life becomes again the earth's joy

And never put back that book, the one there in your hand
The one that I command
Tonight

It is the token that you gave to all those sneering boys pretending
   to be men
Along the shore that you left long ago, and like a dream you con-
   tinue to be a child

When they have died, when they have destroyed their home

When you made it

When you breathed

The air that surrounds the high-cropped sky song alee

Then you became like the end

Concrete Oceans

That numbness never leaves you, only remains
Like a wisp of cloud on a sunny day
And within every single piece of joy
Is a shadow remembering

Because when you open that sunlit door
When you remember who it was for
When the letter you wanted to write
Is driven away like a horse in the night

You take some kind of medicine
That falls before the victory of silence
And slices open this foggy veil
Which rings like truth, golden and stale

And in the morning there are a thousand people standing

In the remains of a house built with wishes

Come meek, come fair
Come seek for what makes you care
Come build and resist the night
Come find it

A glance and you are placed
In the middle of people who are acting out of love
Out of shame, out of the dusk, which falls because
You wish it

And after that moment has passed away from you
There is nothing left for you to grasp, and you are left against the
    burning lights
With a hand filled with innocent seeds of a perfect world

And as the night descends around you, you think of a place
Where you could see her face
But now, as you sit with legendary sadness only felt in dreams
You feel that you could find it, now

She held his hand as they walked on concrete oceans
Looked desperately into this growing mist that you so wish
Would lead them to kiss

But it drowns them out in muted sounds, watches
As grateful men plead for their lives in the dusk

As beauty loses ground, loses its stake in the gamble of time

Lives Were Lives Before

You will always be in the same places
Long after the others, with their crude gestures and wiling glances
Have passed the glass and have moved into the world

You will linger, for a moment, as the final candle is
Put out
On the chandelier of love

You will dwell as you would with the company of merry souls
Chiding the darkness, boding ill to the passing of time

And when their bright colors like forgotten leaves of light
Desist

There will be some faint voice crying out against the pale, opaque
Christening of the morning

I love the end, I love the way
I love the things you bring to stay
I love the calling, so humble in dark
I love the blissful coiling maker of heart

And within what you breathe
A note, so sweet
Within what you see
Nothing

And the tables are set, the chandelier
Of love
Begins to come to you in the next day, as though

Lives were lives before

And what you can do, what you can see

Always comes back to haunt me

In the very same methods

In which you were me.

Walk

I try to disarm what's inside
But, faithfully like a bomb it decides
What you want is what you hide

Deep in what is mind

There is a fathomable notion ringing mighty
But it runs too quickly with the trembling starlight
And it brushes up against the eyelash of the night
And you find it is gone

Quickly move through the ending
Find glisten in the nothing
Bring again your love, in ending
You know that it was for you

The mysterious
Walk

I feel that you know how deep it is
I feel you want to taste it
But you dive down, and like a sound
Move with sorrow's ever-dripping gown

It goes down, down
Swallowed in the sound
Down, down
Swallowed in the sound

Make the love of the ground, come
Beneath it
And drench upwards the fountain that you've dug so mercilessly

Blue is the color of deepest fair
Blue is the winter of the deepest care
That is found in the wonderfully lost

Secret of it

I know there is a place for you

But I can't find it

It cheers its lonely heart for you
You, the diamond I don't know

And the crust digs deep in sideways in waves
The sides of your vision
And the rusted orange wet burst of your sunset heart

Calls
Against
Tomorrow

Evil Luck

I felt my power come back
In the winter shade of a window
In the grasp of a soldier

Who forgot my name

I want you to empty out
And bring your heaven clout
And bring your totem of your lord

It will do you no good

Because tonight they are singing
The bells of nothing
Tonight they are ringing
Ancient songs
A-winging down on the happiness that you thought
You found
Inside the blistering of slanted tomorrows

You live here, yet you do not know
That there is another place for you to go
That there is another time for seeds to sow

That there is love

That there is a place
In the dungeons of your hollow face
That brings to bear the mysterious fare

Of a gift for you, my birthed night

Yet you do not see it
You cannot touch its empty grayness
And like an apple moves with wisdom

So you mock my lightness, here

Never make
Never take
Never leave this wretched place

I love, I live, the gift I give

Is of the fairest quell of that solemn spell

That you wished could bring you ecstasy
And for it you danced fervently beneath your stars
But the stars, the stars

They were not ours

They did not pass into forgotten hours

They shined forgotten, what is shine

What is this mongrel you've brought to dine

On the lusted cup of evil luck

This botched brew of ended time.

Take My Hand

What beauty lies
What, quick, reviles
At the touch of monstrous hands
At the quickened flight of sands

The wretch sneaks behind the bush
With camera, and such
And threatens with shaking teeth
To destroy what it is you seek

I can feel inside your eyes
Calypso, by and by
I can see inside your head
I can find it

The thing that you wanted from the start
The thing that could steal your heart
A voice calming after dark
Of love

Do you want to know the secret
Do you want to heal your past
Do you want to touch heaven
Do you want to drink that glass

Well then, I cannot help you
I come from other design
I come from makeshift ensign
I, from love

Did Shakespeare write an ode
So beautiful and betrothed
To any heart
That wasn't true

Then if, per chance
You smoke and you dance
You cry at the chance
Of revolution

Then sister take my hand
Then sister you understand
That it's I whom you command
Tonight, my love.

Fooled

There is no way for you to know
What comes out of people's mouths and how it relates

To their thinking, because if some man spoke to you and gestured

There would be a wave on some ocean that no one sees

I don't feel like I can exist for much longer, said he
I don't feel like I can go on being the thing that everyone

Hates

Which is only just a wooden face given up to a small once power-
     ful child behind

A football bleacher

They were wearing hats behind me, they were looking through
     the rain and seeing

That I was not their friend, but they can't cut you down, they can't
     know

From the voice that they themselves sowed

Where their mistakes could be.

I can't throw a coin without it landing in a row because you made the coin

And now everything seems cryptic because you

Fooled

Me

Into wishing that I was dead, but there's nothing in the foreground of a shadow

Except you until I turn

My head

Down that other way where I can only see on a stairway

Some broken hearts and a curled rose of sadness

The Nurse

A light.
Frozen like a sea charm, bristling with rifles
Light.

Shine deep depths of the earth like crumbling paper

Fear makes up her lost-charted dream.

A beggar wants a share of the ocean, but

Speaking is distant near the foot of the

Mountain.

Until the words mean nothing and some sort of

Up-roaring bliss

Sprinkles like rain the golden wishing

Forsaken in morning.

Frozen like time

Frozen like a crooked villa vixen

Magic mixed in

Until I sweat, until sweat becomes

My devil.

Lotuses

You have always worn the same clothes
And pausing to light a lamp in the door-way

Was like finding a chisel of sky making designs on your
        dream-bed

Designs like lotus diamond crystal visions, green and black and

With some colors of orange and bliss

But tomorrow you forgot it, forgot to write it down, or else

Speak it to a stranger, and something happened to you then, you
        went down through

A hall made by your lantern-weave, succumbed thieving wishes
        of your

Cut-out light

And throughout the night, through the missing carnivores which
        ate up
The morning when you forgot to do it
Came to me bright and fluid with anchors that held down
        containers

Of lotuses

And then a spider of the brightest wish, because with eight legs
    there are more chances to

Fall fall fall the rhyming murdering withdraw of
Seventy notes of handkerchief raindrop
Which you paid for in your hour, when they came for you, in the
    tears of your making

I don't know what else to give you, the person who forgot it
You left it crying on a doorstep of a strong-armed star, which like
    the sun only more
Only more distant, groped in your being and snatched a leaf of
    lighted missing

Mischievous kissing

And the growling hungry nature that brought you to the door

Then the sliver of daylight disappears
Instead of vanishing, which you thought you could

Make it do.

I Know

You walk out into the naked night
And follow along the jagged dangerous ends of streets

Thinking it would be easier just to be drunk instead

But you realize that when you spoke earlier, there were secrets
which you couldn't allow

There were things you couldn't say to a friend
And when you walk along those other-place streets in the naked
night

You wished that you could have flown away along them in your
imagination
And like a child's peace it becomes broken with the passing of
days days days

Forgetting the nights

But when you walked along the danger street you knew there was
no going back, and
The reality of the soft concrete beneath your conquer-shoes

Bled of death

Sometimes you wish you could stop it but you can't escape, it
haunts like villainy does
The preacher

It haunts like majesty does the broken man jesting, forthright and
	pious questing

By the tearless night

And you again my friend it haunts in passing not caring about its
	coldness

Those jagged streets, in their flight, become where you wished
	you could have been
When you walk exactly on them that night

Flourishing through the changing of the American guard, which
	is more like watching
Streetlights come on at night while driving by them

But you wished you could have walked into the street which was
	dangerous because
You were not drunk

Thinking again where you wanted to be, everything around you
	becomes invisible, and
Instead turns into the majestic villainy of being alive in a place
	where you will never
Where you won't dream while awake

It breaks you before telling you "I knew and I know"

I knew and I know, you laugh to yourself as you quickly hide in
	the shade of night
Which was easy to do
But you still
Can't
Escape

Because the streets that you were walking on were made by some-
	one else, and you can
Only wonder at their beginnings

So you founder for your hip flask Christ flash makeshift weap-
    onry the nighttime jagged
Edge of dreams

And you cut through the end of night, which only made you
    wonder again at something

Opal

I saw planet earth from the bottom step of stairs
And the shadow that cut diagonally across my vision separated

Like the azure distant clouds

Itself

And with it, with time and the making of backwards hands, there
    was in the cloud
A distant rumbling of the future

I looked up from my sitting place
A wrecked place on an untouched shore where I had touched down
Many times
In dream
I saw
It
Breathing with the flying magnificence of the dawning of green-
    vision slightness
That when you hold the flower, just so

You can see through it like the opalsight whitewashed water sky

And with it, with you, my friend it brings you down and you can
    see clearer now in

Your thinking and your vision, because the earth, it said, this
    planet

Is a sphere and circles have no end and so neither does the planet
When thought about in this fashion, and the universe, in turn,
    must be a circle

Because when you got up and walked up the stairs from that
    wrecked ship sitting place

And ascended, you could see, through the azure cloud, striking
    the afternoon with

Dazzling perfect fleets of memories

For a moment, at least, you could walk up and see down what the
    earth looked like

And she was there with you at some time and that was all you
    needed, to see it

Because now you can also see it, and jot it down, sketch you
    thinking because it won't
Much like fear, go away, instead will grow more permanent
    sometimes

Sometimes, like the opal waves of the imagination, of the think-
    ing pattern that did

In time

Bring you to wreck your ship on that island and hunt for the
    child, the friend, the earth

What You Wanted

You traverse by moonlight
And leaving the bent street-light

You fathom in a long way ahead
What it would have been that you had decided

But what you decided was not to go with them, who sat begging
        in the
End phrase of the quickened ghoulish, the crooked and foolish
Light on the altar

Of the night, the streetlight, instead you decided to
Go along with the blond invisible companion, that moon

She wept with you and you thought you had a place for a good-
        night, a tended to firelight
But in the moonlight is where you saw her last and made her tell
        you what it was

That the car that flew through the streetlight momentarily had
        been doing

And again you traverse, the victory is near, the bending bowing
        car that silently

Took them away, silently bore a face and in the moonlight

Against the streetlights, moving quietly alone, you found out

Sometimes I wonder when they would be coming back, she says,
    saying nothing

Of the bitterness of cold other places, the night-stripped faces of

Where you can dream, but leaving again, leaving now

In the moonlight, near the street-light

Is the beginning of your traveling, is the beginning of what you
    wanted to make
Out of her and you realize what it was you wanted to make out of
    her

It was—

It was tomorrow, it was pitched in the newsroom, it was, in time,
    forgotten

But in the moonlight, your dearest moonlight

She was

Layers of Smiles

Silent paper movements
Sipping sand
And lost enchantments

I went back yesterday to the place where I put my keys
And I found out that what I looked at from the face of yesterday
    was somewhat
Like today, although I was older

Grimacing into the fountain of youth, you starkly laugh and point
    like the black
And
White
Paper

That you found you laid to rest with heaving sighs of dirt that you
    used to carry
Around with you, and sometimes put on your feet in hopes of
    seeing

What it would be like when you were at last covered all up in it

No, I don't mean death at all, but rather

The interruption of memory

Because memory is what made you, and memory is who you are, and if you lose
Sight of memorials along that road where you got that bag of dirt, you cheap

Then you'll see that it was in forgetting where beauty was

Coming back down around you are the wings of an angel made in a video game
And slight grimaces made on a television

Then if you counted all the wrinkled faces you saw on the television screens throughout
Your life

Then it would happen so that they would cover your body and make your skin into layers
Of
Smiles

Which is grotesque, until you see what is really behind faces anyway

You will be buried with a photograph of yourself watching television

Because lifting up toward the sky is what made you doubt it, is what made you founder

In the enchantments you were born with and will never go away unless you choose
To somehow send them away, where their ghosts will take the place of what is really there

Which cannot be moved ever.

Awakening

Draw me in with a pen
Across the boards that run across your life
And decide, then

What you made in taking the time

I went back to the place where you wanted me
I went back across the livid chapters of sweet-song bereavement

Of an original piece of something which you could have made
    had you been

Had you been alive

And what else might you find, because the boards, these planks of
    sadness
Which make up how you view me, are rather pieces of debt to the
    twilit sky

Pieces of shadow remembering

And naked on the meadow are masked affectionate liars, lost and
    airborne criers

Which made you plastic under the weight of longing

And the pen which bade you fix in some portrait of me, left out-
    side the lines
The very lines which you contrived

A feeling

And after you go around down that way where you put me in
    there
Where you put me in the prisons of the mind, you might just find

Solace

Solace, for yourself, solace and inside these designations is a dif-
    ferent kind of death

Solemn and precise and without the excitement which leaves you
    on your very day of

Awakening

Color and shape cannot make a face without a word so kind to
    pare its real being

Fixing clean
Its old beginnings

So with the ending meadow which you thought you would die
    on, you bring back some

Some old, some fragmented parcel of being, which takes its turn
    believing

In futures, in the next day, like the moonrise on the forgotten
    quay

Of your imagining

True

They asked me about my weekend
Trailing endings from within their fake gypsy clothes

That they bought prematurely at a capitalist yoga

And there was something I wanted to tell them, but the night is
    dark in the day
The night means nothing when it is hidden like some undersea
    machine

That wins every race and is folded up beneath the earth with
    gems but more

Complex

The night is dark in the day
Make my wishes go away
Think only of what you'll say

In the nothing remembered through a glass

And in this glass there was an undersea day commanded by
    gypsies actual

I wanted to go there when I realized that I was already there, and
    on some vacant
Backdrop canvas of outer space there was a planet wrong with its
    demanding

I knew there was something wrong, and inside my mind was the
    sunken day
The loved way of the gypsy keepers of a place where you could go
    with everything

True

It was a polygamist of sunshine that brought you away from me,
    love, and left me

Sitting darkly

In the folded up parts of the night-day-wrong-way scratching
    throated mystic

That turned into something that I realized gave it two different
    meanings

Like when you sat on a red bench and the end of the world
    happened

And gypsies keep the day-clock
They wring out the sun
They always make it so you run
Run like ghost houses and a folded sideways dream

You must hurry up now, you must make haste and close the door
    to the garden of the
Dead woman

You must run quickly away from the ghost gypsy making love
    between the
Sacrilege fold of what lurks in your mind between night and day—

Between sorrow and love

Oceans

Remember where you used to dream
And there was a diamond sunset reflected in the sea
And there were places which reminded you of me

Breathing quietly by the sea

Forget what you may have already known
That the love you find is the one you've shown
Deep down and that you've always known

Would come find you

There are thousands of silent voices beyond that screen, there
Bring with you a basket of light to the top of the stair
And inside what you'll find, dear, what you'll find, my love

Is that there was once something

I know that you don't take this seriously
I know that there is something else that you wanted to find
But isn't the truth we once knew enough?

No,

Never hide, never smile
Against the hidden caves of yearning
Never wish, never give

Yourself more chances than you need

Remember when you used to dream
There were mountains, and on a mountain-top
Crowned with lightning and green trees, overlooking into the
    gasping valley of sunlit

Oceans

Where you could always find what you came for
Then there is an awakening
A new changing of the guards of heart

And it closes up, you open your eyes

And see its ending

Before you go tonight
Back to your chambers of wishing
There will be a thing you'll need to remember

Beside the places you used to dream

Tonight.

Mirth

I hear another wishing
Brought down from the opening
That still opens when you close it
That still belongs to hearts frozen

Can you not go away?
The singer bows and the slighter stays
For the ending wish, the darkened scheme

Of another hope flying desperate

I crashed upon the daylight found
Wrinkled in a basket
I ran then, to another day
And inside a house, I found it

It was sleeping, drying out mismatched clothes
And singing, "let the child in"
I can't return, it makes and burns

The breaking of a chime

In which
You see
I find
Them free

And the blossom of the church where you bring
Your pious mirth

It is a place, lit frequently and in a daze
By streetlights, neon sacred ways

The flowing of the day
Is not so silent

And blocking my view is a forlorn
Ending of sorrow

It rubs against the sun and wishes that it was done

Because it is, my friend, your hoping

Fragile

It would have been better for a woman to sing the song

But there is a bus driver in an empty bus that is waiting for

Children

And the bus is parked in the mist of the day, which is fragile
   when you really see it
When it's fragile and you seem to miss it

As you fall away fleeting

Because through the window of the vehicle are thousands of
   thoughts moving
Like the sun

And the day becomes something you can see through, the mid-
   day light is now

Just like it sometimes is

Without a shield

And moving through the roads which the bus driver has already
   seen

Are the flocks of waiting children missing a small sliver of heart
     as they are hoarded

Onto misguided buses, yellow thin obstructions to their dreaming

What did you see
When you lifted a finger and rolled over in bed by yourself, did
     you see it
Did you see yourself, no

It was too dark and the way the next day came was like misery
     but you saved a piece

Of your past dreaming so that when you awakened you could
     remind yourself of the

Liars

And I don't want you to know what I think sometimes about
     them
I don't want you to fathom how much I care about nothing, and
     until you drive

A bus through the streets filled with nothing but the intersections
     of lines of vision
Coming from every other car, and every other once-child who
     had ridden on it

That you can finally see what it was you forgot to bring with you
     to the field trip

And sometimes when a girl you once remembered that was unat-
     tainable slips through the
Cracks and
Gives you
A reason to

Forget

You don't want to and instead think of all the messed up things
    that you went through

And see it as the day becomes more fragile

Fragile, as in a corner store unused might be if someone saw it
    from their

Childhood, and the bus drives by it, and you remember just once

That song that girl sang for you some time ago.

Of Words

That paradise you call home
With the light from day slanting in through unused rooms
Unused for sewing, or other joy-ridden things, and then

Something about how the day went by and you didn't notice the ligl

Made you think about how often there should have been a girl

Someone there to give you something, a tree-reaching crow call
From the back end of the room where you smoked, and the light

It was too frail because it was winter and you were alone, somehow

Belligerent other callings from other walks
The stiff regimented sadness
The way you wished you had something that talked
Besides a memory of a another room filled gladly

And you dismiss how fragrances of women were missed from you
    inner chamber

I don't know how much more happy you would have been, but
    sinking deeply into
The light of an unused day, you proudly and without purpose forg
    to have
Fun at age twenty four and those women that you always give out
That you always talk to and never form meaning with bathed you
    the sound of light

Which was just a memory, dripping with the callus inward
    dreaming that you said, and

The paradise of home is just another wasted space for you to
    think about how
When you leave the place you were born and make a new one,
    how far it really was

How far you really had to fly on rooftops and quickly lit sunrises
    you missed
To show you how ridiculous the room could have been with an
    old fashioned sewing

Sewing of words, sweet perfume and the dismissal of the burning
    lights of night, the
Streets sallow and curdled in their wish to be in a home

And an uncouth driver of dreams bellows strongly in the silence
    and you wished for
Crows and a cowboy hat man to bring you back to a day when
    sewing clothes instead

Of words

Was relevant to you, but Montana is not a gift
It is a deletion of the sinful city breath that bade you grimace at
    its prospects

So you wasted it on a boy with a large heart

But knowing where to begin is over now
Just like tomorrow you might look into the unused room and see
    a ghastly image

Of what it was that sewed your heart with flowers, and, and,
    sometime, and nothing

The cowboy hat burning under a darkened city painting that you
     stole from gods
That gave you lips to untie madness, to drink in glad watermelon
     fields and to lose

What just left you there instead of saying something that would
     have made those sewn
Rooms
Glad

Color Mechanism

The end of the sky, lavender grandeur
Crocheted at the end of a part of the road

I wanted to meet you in an anime
I wanted to meet you in the 1950s in a small town romance
I wanted to love you

It's true, I do

Sometimes you wander out into the night and you don't know
      where you're going
You wander lost and courageous and filtering through a storm
      cloud is purple

Believing nothing you chalk it up to a name card that you gave to
      the jewel

That secret part of the end of the night road, and you

Wished for the making of something larger or more important
      why did you make me

Leave you

It does work out, it does come eventually, said the harangued cut
      and plastered color

Box

Color

Mechanism

You stole from me, you cheated me out of what I thought love
  would be
You saw into me, you saw deeply the cheapened dream of the end
  of a skyway believing

And

I know it, you did, I saw the broken shells of a glass covering of a
  portrait I gave that

Stuck up from the suburban coffee-house themed kitchen floor
  that was a pale wood and
Which gave your stubborn face the color of a black fridge with a
  picture of Mr. Insane

On it, wearing a box color red jacket

Then

I drove down the road and in the sound of the storm connived
  and broke again the same

Picture

Because it was only a picture

Crocheted in the end of August leaving in a storm cloud a piece
  of me

In a piece of the heart that moved you along that road that you,
     that you, that you

Made

That it seemed to make in your heart a smooth glass re-doing of
     the portrait of yourself

Lost lavender hangs around your night-memory like a woven bit
     of paper you . . .

It's true, you did.

Pennants

He took the evening train at twenty-six and reached nirvana at
   twenty-seven

How many times have you seen him
How many pieces of gallant stinging rays have been through him

How many times has he been caught alone?

There were beams of fire coming from the basketball crowd
I marched in with the bass amp, and the point guard reported me
   to the police of souls

Wherein I was sent away, away down into the depth

You placed in that part of the heart where there is a place for a
   fixture
A plain many rosefield fixture, with glowing bulbs of saffron and
   jade wind, mixed with

The smell of ocean in your hair

Sometimes I wonder somehow how you became that fixture

But I think now that because you were there can be no archer for
   my heart

I took down all those things, those flags and treasure maps on my
    secret other door room
And burned them with fire from a bass amplifier, laughing cor-
    dial jade emulsifier, pennants

Worn alone

Travel down with me to the train station, which glimmers like a
    faded antique lamp that has not
Been lit

In twenty-seven years, and then you'll know how it is to bleed all
    over the deck of a ship
How it is to command those wretched grievance-bearing salt
    water revengers

I noticed deeply how your eyes moved away from the evening
    light on the evening train

But I forgot to write you a letter from hell, like I so often did,
    painted red, red red rainbow

And stabbing in the dark, which was like light all over except
    more plain and comfortable

I found the place where my heart could have been pierced and
    with a flourish and epee

Disfigured it, so that now when I travel long distances

I miss where the train line ends and the train goes out into the sea
    and I think of a star thief
Missing his place, where I gladly tell him that I wore his shoes
    alone when he was gone, and

That it does exist on the days that matter, which is enough

Costumes

Why am I here
Why did you leave

I kept a darkened door for you
I kept a long line of lost again

Matches and used up ends of thoughts
And some time ago you drew on my heart a coarse mesh of maps
    and
There was a kind of foolishness where
You ran naked believing in the light the night its all the same

Except when in some fever the tendrils of your end-time grab
    hoarsely at the image
Of your past dream, so you clothe yourself in the rain-soaked
    droplets of lost love,

Lost plans and quietly crafted machines that build up an end

It became with you common to be cruel, matchbox paper fools
    and false lovers in hooded

Costumes

Coming for the image of you in a small shallow pool, the ends of
    thoughts burned up like
Grayness in your heart and it stood up,

It beckoned to you and you lost your dream, your crooked
    stitched knitting made of last year's
Calendars

And there was a calmness in
Your child,

You gave it to the night and the
Colors escaped like how you
Could have been here

And the door opened and you forgave nothing, it swept you
    inside the room which was

Gray and pungent with loneliness, so you shut down the door,

Failed at matches, and moved away

Don't go, they might say, don't go

They said.

Give In

He borrowed part of the flesh of the horizon and left another
    night out to dry

The sky a charm the smoky horizon of trees,

I think that perhaps I can

Nothing in the works, the year is rebirthed scattered narrations of
    the prisoners of dusk,

Endless dust, a rhythm in the stillness

I know you made a way for me
I know you were there but the sea is far away and like butchered
    dreams you clean the sallow
Long fought-for kitchen and you draw ages on the water,

It comes alive to you and what you thought you needed was a
    calamity to wake you from the day

Begin, end, renew, mend

It's all the same to me

Decide, begin, lose touch, give in

This begotten entrail of me this star trail, and now it seems

Just like it used to seem

Except it's a different century, a different hour I count rhythms in
    the feeble feeling
Of your parched and bleeding mouth, your hands holding hearts
    over a fire

Whose?

Then the destruction is no longer what you needed and love like
Some disease breaks across the sky and there are no more dark-
    ened trees,
Just the end of something

So Badly

She had Tom Waits wrapped around her waist like a sword belt
   and the bad rain

Came, marching through the freeway tunnel
Fizzing until it lit a spark of loneliness in a passing car and yes you

Went that way alone,

You encountered the conversation of the two enraptured lovers,
   his hips on his and you

Somehow

Became sick with the night because there are no heroes this time
   around
Charm, swell this blistering dream

And hatred was not an American thing and you knew that some
   patronizing fool was
Running for the offices like a clap-bell diver, the mistaken cadaver
   of the lonesome and so you

Finished it and went out where the souls were

Reaching into the snowy unknown and death, sweet voices of an
   untamed thrall and you wished

So badly

That she was with you

The wind on prairies said goodbye, sometime sailors and their
  wistful cries and you weren't

Buried alone, just again with the pirate graves, inside the hills
  remembering,

Never mind she said it's just the—

Someone You Once Knew

You do know you sated the captive making morning with your breath and you washed your hearse in a bikini in the Blair dairy Queen drive through I know you you got fed up and dated a teen idol and grappled unsuccessfully in some night at a dream resort near the Bay area and something you once said about bottle cap fortunes and stealing cigars from the movie store made me want to keep the same hours as most of the living but your love soured in the darkness, it reared an invisible head and brought you back to the high school fool school beckoning South facing prison and you didn't see the condoms sometimes in the parking lot and you didn't realize it was the result of either a Texan prostitute or your famed idol but also you may have made friends

With the prostitute vicariously through someone you once knew, and eventually they kept talking about it on the radio because no one said anything

Love Was

Captive mornings release them to me destroy intrepid believing

I want

The feeling of a rescinded ephemeral chain against some
Kind of pasture dream

Replete with home grown flowers the flowers were home grown
    and you looked

Into god's face and noticed they were all darkened in the moonlight,

You couldn't see them, they recoiled briefly from your touch and
    wandered centuries away
There was nothing at the end of the road
The lost moonshine girl and some bastard shotgun boy

They turned away and made a chapel against what you called a
    morning so

You left out the back door into the new city and captured a picture
    of flowers and love was

A graveyard that you went to in bliss and sacrilegiously destroyed

You broke and recoiled them and what was in the dream were oceans

I Too Will Not

What wind is this
Draping silhouettes

It clatters through the yard, and
There was an escaped prisoner beckoning for his rights with his
    left hand,

Nothing came between him and the storm
I looked him in the eye and some story was told, after which it
    was forgotten

You can't make the same day twice, they said, but the night is
    different

The yard contained a fragment of a bed tossed from an attic-floor
    apartment

It bled consistently with the moon
It crossed over, it held its breath and waited for the endless arrow,
    the thin scrape
The jewel

I don't know what I did with the jewel I don't know where I lost it
    I don't know

I don't know

Just where I lost it, where I put it out of sight, and some text mes-
     sage annihilation moment

I kept it for myself, I think, which was the problem, and by now

The prisoner is escaped, free in the world to roam and do what he
     pleases with his flowers
I can't control it, or him, or you, they said to me.

Let me confide in you your deep secret, that I do know
Let me whisper in low tones beside the chandelier in the chamber
     of the empire
Let me point with a gladdened smile and turn in so you'll hear
     me above the noise:

You want love

And then there will be no turning back for us, the football team
     perished in hell, one by one
And the basketball team perished in hell
And the track coach burned in hell what is this flower I've
     forgotten

Am I so luxurious now that I think that I too will not

Grasp my hand, Death, because you are near me, much like an
     orgasm drains the sap

Drains out my body, I know there is some kindred spirit of the
     lonely eye, because when
She looked
At me, she cried

And away down the mountain rambled the prisoner, still holding
     a scar of the door

Still carrying the tattoo of the moon, and then

Forget it, forget everything because it had nothing to do with you

The Same As Praying

The mystic power of your words haunted the trespassers
Until they were weary, until they were done

And what happened to the gun left you numb wondering

I can't go there now, anymore, or before, now
I can't bleed any more

Something tells me you're down, though, seeped through with
     the power

And the nothing short of magic night swept you off the floor, and
     carried you through

Some blisteringly simple honky-tonk where you died and envi-
     sioned your dreams

But that doesn't have to be now, you know it isn't now
It doesn't have to be what you wanted, either, even now, even now

I came upon a village destroyed by the body politic and wept for
     the pagan sunlight
I wept, which is the same as praying only more beautiful, and I
     saw you

At least, there among shambles and other white men, because the
  instantaneous relationship
That we had as strangers can't be exposed unless you talk about it,
  which then leaves it

Decayed and scarred, like the charred remains of Bethusela

What's left to dream? Some dram, some scream

Some pittance for the end, and the clock that took you there

I reiterate not for my sake but yours:

Don't go

And what was on the radio was nothing, so you shut it off and
  became like love for a moment

In all the wrongness of your words, I noticed impossibly the
  beauty in your silence and silent
Hands

And you moved your head to the side and slowly blinked and I
  saw light

You're not down anymore, and instead I beg you to not go where
  the radio goes

But to renounce the powerless and lay claim to what is rightfully
  yours, a cherished womanhood

Of complex beauty and sadness, which like the trespassers, were
  alike

Infinitesimal

Then you'll lose all your courage and dance away

Just like some sign by the road advertising beer

I feel now in my dying moments that it wasn't so bad, as they say
It wasn't so bad

This will be my last poem because after this I will kill myself

Unless I can find a way to rhyme

She touched your shoulder and sent a dagger into your soul, a
    dagger because you knew
You couldn't have it, and then as you felt dried up,

It is in saying your death that you meld death and life into one
    experience
You beautiful chance, your dancing neon smiler beside the end of
    your other road

It wasn't so bad to see the sign or anything else, you felt, because
    you were cruel to yourself
And
Declared
Death

A declaration of death can stop it—say you are dead now, life breede
Say death's name as you whisper coyly to your imaginary love un-
    der a purple nightsign

Then suddenly coming back to you is all the words you could have
    said, which was your poem

Shut up the door, shut it up out loud and

Declare infinitesimal

You are on the other side of death so you can say whatever you
    want, now
You've taken your revolver medicine, so jump into the window wi
    the lilacs

And her hand, a slight missed sweetness, landed on your back and
    you felt impossible
Because she was the one you loved, and would

You counted words beside the coffin of your love and decided that
    instead you were all dead

You were all lifeless in the nightsign morning, you were all dancin
    around the grave
Of cowardice

And bravely you sought out the man on the mountain so he could
    die, instead

Vices of Woe

In the bold night a man walked across his freedom
Believing in the chained dream of the smoke downstairs, the
    armored chairs

Statues beholden to his love

I crumbled in that doorway, that forbidden way, that enclave of
    sheltered woe

That miscreant of the endless throe of
What heart you held in your hand, there

I mistook it for the bell which I traveled with, the sound of seas
    and how you fooled me
How you deem and how you dream of the
Vices of woe

I, we, they, then they say, just to be
Just to live free is where long shadows
Armed clavichords that play the grave

I clamber into the hearse and what you heard is the bell-clap
    mystery beckoning southward

Chambers and summoning dangers from the gem-ridden sea that

Sees you seventeen and
Makes you belong to the crumbling fashioned
Parlor of psychedelic Tannenbaums

How you say ghost in German beckoned me to your sleeping
place, but not there and so I
Slip down into the freedom and crawl along songs toward the forest

Love forest, love plain, love deep and
Disdain covered up within the group of unidentified stars in the
untouched hours of grace

And forgetting to heat the night, it snows dreams in your past
What was your glass you gave them?

When did those eyes, red specks at the
Modern intersection, piercing through the snow

Gentle and deadly they christened armchairs in the dust

Old Fashion

I paid $150 for a ghost
That left me stranded along Broadway in the desert

Don't remember how they were made, just remember them

Caustic lying night, abide
The fiction of the roiling tide
Validate, surmise
How clever was her disguise
How simple was the pattern of death
Written

Noose the day and hang its conspirators beside the

Ramshackle assembly of mirrors that you use to hide in

I cry in the caustic night for the return of a room that I had once
    sat in

I sat in the room, and from the window of that room

From the right-facing properly stitched marquis of the fallacy of
    confidence in a ghost I

Remember a blue haze sky and a peaceable corner with a white
    chair and a brown table

The saturation of hatred bottled between the sun-rays the
Endings of the song which had made the place, and the ending of
    the rain which signaled

A rainbow across hell

Located in the two story brick building just south of the hospital

Disguises of faces bring you to the plot of land where you wanted
    to fuck

And within laughter is the signal of how happiness ends, just like
    gold mongers, who
Like grueling scarecrow men board the sunrise and claim to have
    some several bits of it

In their pockets like jangled gems and otherwise lost Spanish
    pieces of life

Because they said the Spanish sun was the best, and the French
    moon, and the Italian gypsy

And the American guitar

None of it means what you think it should, none of it cries with
    southward hanging shipsails

The painting on the wall is not as bland as you once thought,
    which is by the brown table
The brotherhood of nothing sits angled on the fence away from
    the window, outside
What you hear outside is the terror that was your decisions, and
    nothing

Ever

Decided, nothing ever shown you knew that fakeness was just the
    signal of

Useless jangle dollars in the ghost-lit sunrise of the past of your
    favorite

And they whisper and they moan
And they diamond and they throne
The end of what you used to be
The very name given
And they tied up the ribbons and they buttoned the bows and

Now, they said, you could be complete with just a touch of cre-
    tonne and some

Miss America honeycomb coffee ground car swallowing darkness

"I know it wasn't you"

Note of Breath

I communed with the dead over telephone
Long lines of gracious memories left abandoned in a dial tone

Long lines of protruding shadows around a hot July room

I wanted you there, tomorrow, when you said you would be there
I wanted everything you put out in the night like a forgotten light

Mysterious flight

Dreams of bygone rooms, changing blooms of shadows around light

I loved inside the room, because it came at me during when I had
    my back turned

It came slightly forward when I had my back against the sun, turned

I know you thought of me sometimes

Yet I remembered that there is always a melodic saying for those
    that are
Forgotten mostly, just remembered thoroughly in small sacred
    moments

Leaving breathless marks on a tired wealthy July afternoon in a
    rich woman's estate
Made up of flowering mistaken steel fence

That rubs without motion against the pale tree-lighted shadows

I need you

Come with me sometime, I'll show you the untouched estate or
    otherwise known
Mansion

Which I sometimes used and sometime past used for commu-
    nion with dead songs

Deceased slain passed away killed murdered let go far away
    drunk to death songs
That could have some words, if the words were long or strong
    enough

But the song is the dial tone and the phone cord is umbilical
    toward my past

I long wish for long ended flourishes of a faint distant note of
    breath
A note of breath descending

And you know I wished for that sweet secret breath
That comes ubiquitously to lovers or friends or a place shielded
    by secrets

But you will be naked in the downturned expression of shadows
    in your lone room

Just like it was for me

Perhaps and by chance you'll go, again

Listening faintly to believe

Slugger

She holds a sign saying "Play rock"
She holds a sign and you drive home again
Again
From some bar where you wanted to speak with more than just a
      whisper, but
Things are different for you now,

Trenches and the bowels of love fly swiftly from the hour, fly
      swiftly from you
Against the murderous backdrop of an empty street, and you feel

The motions of the wretchedness of that mysterious sea that
      dwells within you
And faking poets make the girl with the sign sigh again and again

You don't know how much further you'll have to drive, and
Something told you that from some other time that the result
      would be the same but
In gardens with roses you keep picking up those that others drop
      there for you

You keep picking up secrets like dusted hidden pieces of the coin
      where you get
Both bad ends, and

Playing what she wanted to hear, you disarm yourself and let her
      be alone

Explosions run along the sky and you feel as though this is your
    ending
And you hollow out a space in the trenches where you find that

At the bar, leaning, was

A girl with a sign saying "Play rock"

And you in confused embarrassment wrote several theses

In the trench, where the rockets were other loves and you, friend,
    you

Were their favorite slugger
Their favorite winner of hearts, if only you held on to the bowels
    of the sea

Longer.

Tomorrow is a forsaken word
Tomorrow is the thing you heard
She said I'm going going hearing a leaning
Hearing just what you learned

Some time ago the rhythm left you but now as tomorrow fades
    into yesterday

It doesn't help and somewhere you'll kill the darkness.

Left Away

The road's not there anymore anyway
And when you traveled down it helplessly avoiding the

Emergence of the freezing of memories, you didn't think about how

The road, someday

Would be gone

Cajole the sunrise, make it whisper to you
About what the road was like
Control the fireflies as they circle you in your revelry

Of the past which is really never in control but is out of

Your control, and when the weeping of the stillness of what could
    have been
Some good type of friend, or something more, you think of all the
    songs

Your footprint in the sounds

Never speaking aloud again, it will be bulldozed and will crumble
    up beneath the
Water of another world, helpless begging of your old lover girl

You wasted and breath-fed other woman
That you loved when you used to drive, hand out the window,
    reckless in your love
State, in your love chime and charm, which rhymed and harmed
    you again when you

Left away

But to stand there and say, as the road is a pile of mud, a long
    streak of mud through
Plow fields

You remember alike those sweet and starry nights, those grim
    and forward moving
Helplessness-killing, October-bringing
Raiders of song, and you became in the most beautiful way

What you needed to be, but now the road is gone, it's been torn
    up anyway
And like the frozen memories with it

Thaws when you don't see it, thaws when it is in peace, and songs
    like water
Drip from the sun, curing it

You Made It

You see the city by night
And throughout each of your musings, alone by the riverside

You find out how many times she killed you
Because now, when you've grown older and away from the vine
    laden itch for it
You can have better memories now in your twenties when you
    look for it

That peace of it that left you somewhere along the vine
And it grows, matching souls, drawing out the feeble throes of the
    galloping
The hallow thing the open-minded sunrise

Within and without each breath of doubt you somehow found
    where
Within the scope and without hope to bear
You
My friend, my unknown crumbling, grumbler throw-away

Have brought the light of skyward vines to mind today

But they don't have a building and then start growing on each
    other and

Like lovers are forgotten, until someone digs them up from the

Eastern bliss and with a kiss renounces their vows, their hidden
    vouchers and

Sullen blows to the wind

Each having its own chapter you fix up a book about when you
    knew

There were thirteen ways to escape heaven and hell, until you
    bristle with the
Nonchalant knowledge of the past lover that wasn't yours, and
    isn't yours anymore

Even though it was you, then

And now, along the ploughs of the sky there are vines growing,
    minds sowing
For the future, for those children you may have had

And in the bliss for the end of the day is just the same as the
    beginning of the day except

You made it

Throughout those breaths of doubt is a rhythm you can't discern
    because ancient relatives
Of your thinking

Kept busy and didn't think about doubting until they died, which
    is when they became

Like vines
Forgotten

My Friend

It's not going to happen that way because of the way you dreamed
It's not going to happen at all, and then you'll forget to speak as
    some

Demons and songs churn your inside out

Because

There is something inside that is like a lake of blood with a figure
    coming out of it
That makes you want to curl up and desist from the world of
    waking
But you cannot because only the moments before when you first
    start sleeping

Do they haunt

A song is not a rhythm but the idea of a rhythm, and a rhythm is
    nothing more than
A heartbeat

And a heartbeat has just now passed you by, has just now left you
    wondering

Why it didn't happen that way

Take peace in the beginning of your thinking, because it doesn't

Matter

It doesn't matter too much, my dear, how you think it, but rather
How you feel

On that lake which is only inside your mind, in some unused
        place of discarded passions
Can you only find the monster that made it

I will tell you about the monster that made it but first love me
        gently
Love me dear
Love me and hold me and whisper in my ear what
You longed to say to yourself when you were a child, because
        now, because ever

The wishing that never happens, only becomes in your thinking

Because you made it, you made a lake of fear in your mind, which
        sits undisturbed

In the bottom of the world, in the unlit lake in a cave
Of your heart

Which only, which only, which only makes it so
That flowers can't grow, and

That figure rising up is you
Until you move about in the world and make a plan for yourself,
        you don't realize

What kind of straw-bed leisure torture you made in your past,
        and then you look down

You look down and with a cracking voice say nothing

Only write it down, and look in your pocket and find a ripped up
    scrap of past love

And unchain your dream until it becomes three-dimensional and
    rattles its bones
For a moment, until the peace is restored and you

My friend

See it face you and die in some oblique way, face you and die

Like you knew it would sometime anyway.

Tangled Spirit of Longing

You wanted to be safe at home
When your home was lying to you

About how it could be made into a place to escape dreaming

And what you saw flying upwards across the banister

Of the winged dreams of the sky

Was nothing more than a ragged jagged wish
You made long ago

And when you returned home, after some grief
After some displacement of being

You saw the stars encompassing it
Lose their meaning

Until you rose up out of the water, the water of the

Tangled spirit of longing

And you made a new way through the fading halls of streets with
buildings

The faded halls of the night's poisoned gift of itself through the street

And when you rambled drunkenly home in a dream

You found the meaning of the dreams of the sky, flying

Upward across some vision you had of a girl, a lover you never
    loved drinking wine

On the promenade of a Paris street

And flinching slightly at the way that Americans love, you
Put it in your pen, until your mind became diseased until you coul

Breathe it out in silent keyboard clicks,
Silent
Silent waves of the drowning of dreams

In the Morning

If beneath the courageous sky you see
The steeples of heads of wanderers seeking

Fools in love

Then you've come to the wrong place, said the face which put you
    in your place

In the morning

I have everything to give
I have, to ever see
The flight of the steeples rescinding
Again, again

Into the sky

And what with the things you said so mercilessly to yourself
Again
Are the things
And the wishes which bring you from the tide

Momentarily

But when you walk and you see the sharpened shadows of the
    people on the street
In an evening when you thought, in passing, that it was an eve-
    ning nicer than what

You thought it might be like

Then take from me the withering tides hidden

In the morning

And forsaken pieces of that ship which treads lightly along the
sun's disappearance

Playwrights serving coffee to lonely upset women
Sneakers left gently in the snow
Lovers beginning to find a way to listen
And the growing anger festering below

But what is below is not your heart, but rather in the keeping of
the sea

Is the beginning corner of a steeple that instead of making shad-
ows, makes

In the weeping hour

The hands of the clocks which kept you there.

What's On Your Mind

You left in the twilight when
I saw you, still beaten from the morning
And through the glass fountain

I found you

Don't make a way
For thoughts already spoken
Don't choose to stay
With words mute and broken
But rather

In time

Make a way through the dusk

There were another thousand voices on that pier that you made
    in the dust
There were blitzing rowing battlements encased in that morning

But I chose to see you instead, see your leaving and it gave me
With the dread I missed

A hoped glass of truth

But then the next day came, and the next, and after some time
    had passed
I remembered one night how I wanted to leave in the twilight
Because of you

But I didn't know where to look, and the ships all left somehow or
    another during
That day, that downward looking day

So that now when I wake, I always seem to miss and continually
    climb
Upwards to that place where you are dwelling

But there is another half of meaning somewhere behind you
Behind your shadow, apart from you, even the other half of you,
    which is only seen
At night

Because truth is a demon, waiting strongly for light
In the misted forlorn crying of happiness

I want you to say, rather
What's on your mind

What did you do today?

Yet I know too well what you've done today
It's the same as yesterday, the same thing I did

Which is lose some part of soul in the dust-ridden sunrise.

What It Is

If I could only cry for you
When the right time came and the songs like pattered window panes

Gave off the feeling of love

If I could only cry for you
I said some time, I do not know when the right time to cry is

In the beginning I saw a flash of hatred, a flash of something cruel,
    and in

My journey, in my hastening to the truth

I could have forgotten my heart

But the window I'm looking through, the pores of flashing infinity

In the quiet gray vacancy of hopelessness

You give up hopelessness when you gain freedom, and when you gain

Freedom

When you gain that glistening sought for veil, then you forget

Why you lifted up a shade in the morning to reveal your dream of
    your own

Child

Then some angel comes down and you smite them down with you
    hands, because

What returned to you is what made you, crawling monster of the se

Then you lose what it is, what is it, what it is

No cryptic volume or wilting piece of paper, but rather

The feeling of love

And when you forget what to say
As days grow cold along your favorite streets

Opening to the wind is your heart, you forgot your heart

"You forgot to bring your heart!" they will say, but
Empty is the place where there should be tears wetting the window

Know

Gypsy me this, oh beggar of bliss
When you brought down your sacred head

Fiddle me this, oh light and quick bliss
Which was the easy way out

No, no the earth said below
It is not for you to take, you see
Because in the beginning, in the end
You'll find no solace in mystery

Because the words you made were the words that broke you
That tore you
That rent your heart from the sepulcher

And dragged you into a town and showed that your groping

Was repeating what a child said more cruelly

Do not infest the break and brazen fires of the middle of earth

For in the middle of earth may be a painter waiting to paint you
down

On side of road, of liar's tongue

Of gross destruction of the rung

Which you so gallantly made in Spain, in Cortez

Who now drips with the folded voice of nothing in his private
and earthy prison

Become what you are and hold on to it
Become what you think and be near to it
But don't harm with it, don't chide with it

Know

It is now what you know, this love, this burden
It is how we feel, these things, these broken

The bread was tossed into the Seine, and was eaten long ago

By gypsy me this, by riddle me quick, by mountain side sick

Of leaning

Conquer the world and by doing so

Give it up, and give the lantern to those who know more fre-
quently and better openly

What it is and how strength is given and how virtue, in old, may
be returning

On the shore of mystic rambling

On the galloping sunrise unable to by caught by the knower

Wake

I dream through a leaf
And when I dream
The thousand voices shaking
Become unseen

What can you discern from the cloud
With pieces of lead that are filled with dread

Boughs of cotton-thread

I know how to feel you, I know how to taste you but
When the thought of an old king brings me peace

I know you are wrong

It was some time ago when I proved that
Dreams are real

Then they stand up and the unseen makers make
They break and sweat those things for you to take
They push out mingling voices that break

Whate'er it is, whatever it is

That makes the morning so inflated with you

There was a piece of machine that spoke out and in the screen

I saw a face so clear and with a friend mumbled that I would one
	day

Destroy the machine and see the face

But the sea is so wide, it doesn't sleep, the beings and the things
	that dwell in the deep

So if tomorrow is today, and I feel I can pray for

Blistering warmth on a sweet sail

Then, my love, then my dear
It's on that ship that you'll long to hear
The sacred mystery of being near

The cotton-thread dreams of a captain dear

Wake
Wake
Wake
Wake
Wake

The fisherman gleams with no eyes and the beginning of time
Is the end of time
It is not a rhyme, but how you make your feeling

Brush the wind with a painted thin brush

And clean your remembrance like water, which although flows
Doesn't know

How to fake it

Knot

In a quiver of speech you can trim a leech
And make some sense out of time

But making a rhyme for those inclined

Is sin

My favorite day is the day when you come home, because it is
    when

You love me

But flowers grow from the ground and birds make cackling
    sounds . . .

I knew.

I knew how to watch the baneful clock as it smote down your
    maker
I knew how to tie and try to find the beginning of your better, but
    later
When the sun flew down and the moon rose up I saw her, the girl
    who was divine

Who you destroyed and then took the time

To incline

Back I go down through a valley once made golden by your
   speech but I have

Nothing

In a quiver of a moment because something told me that I could
   have saved

The very breath you made

Had I not gone away forever . . .

But tying up the knot

Is the waking truth forgot

In the sweeping of the gesture where I left you

And so tomorrow will be the same, and some day when you're
   aflame

I will pull out a letter like this, exclaim your name

And you will be forgotten just the same

Like a rhyme of seventeen candles
Which I was too late to berate,

Mixing handles

She Missed You

If there was a way to
Send messages through lanterns and fix up chains with ghosts

Then you would do it

But the speech of villains is the speech of lions in the morning
    lantern

And everything you once knew is flying fast, the voices of birds
    and the beginning of

Grumbling voices

Is like the fastening of some kind of coward whisper in the
    middle of a room, naked

And easily they come around you, put you down like a million
    other divinities

Because they broke your back and hung you on planks above the
    sea

Which was never yours

Clear up your mind and see for yourself what you have done,
    because if you wrong

The person that showed you love, then you wronged everything
    that you knew

But live, but listen
The chalked-in forest of city pavements in places
Where voices have spoken and left a linger
Of hatred which spurs on more of it

I know
The way
Where you stay
Is dead, is dead
I can see from the quay
You made for your sister, who when she was with you
    Gave you another kind of love
And she missed you

She put down a piece of paper on a stand by a lamp and turned
    with eyes like frightened
Animals, noticed the way that you cut up a newspaper, and the
    sound that it made

Gave her despair

Because its not in the way that you live

Its in the way that you die that makes the end seem filled with
    happiness, when

The end is only a truth that you can face now rather than
    tomorrow.

Something Moved You

Your feet as you shuffle along the night
Are perfectly in line with the dripping of the rain spout
In the dryness

When you walked out of it, when you walked to the precise
        moment
You felt something, everything, something move
But it was gone

Bring down several pieces of what you wished for then, and care-
        fully plot them
On a line with the rain-spout

I don't know, I do not know
The music that you wished is now down below
Now draw them down, watch them grow
Again

Floating down from the edge of the door that you saw
Is a woman's voice, so quiet and so smooth

Behind the locked door

And inside are several coated men with some kind of letters
Watching for your movements, but they don't know you

And it is reassuring that they don't know how you are as you walk
   against the night
And with it
And with time
And with the rain-spout as the drops keep time with how you are
   walking, you

Look back as several pieces of the night, several dreaming secrets

Wash with the non-existent, smooth-talking rain

She gave you a drink and you noticed very quickly how she
   smiled because she was
Wearing some cheap glasses and the glasses she cleaned were not
   dirty and

Something moved you

But now, as the rain washes down and the men drive away, one
   cannot help but notice

Sweeping angels of the dusted silence of gray earth in that sweat-
   ing palm of yours

As you drink down the water in the glass that came from the
   spout, and you wish

That the pieces of the night that you walked on were enough
That they could have said something else, but
Wait, diamond, wait along the door and I will breathe you in

After the pawns of darkness

Bells of God

Look up, look up
He spoke into his teacup
For the sea is speaking,

Speaking low

And these bustling forefathers of the end cry out in muted fear

Against the waking monstrosity of the night

When you walk down some street and enter some lot with cars

The time between is a gift

And the way you lost your breath that day

Put me down

Hearken to some other thing and put it in your back pocket and
    then
Take it with you as you walk to some shelf and with cheery
    dimpled wicked cheeks
Smile and place it

Go around this crux of light that brings you from sacredness into
    the dark

Some time when the words run dry
Take a gift and place it
Some night when the winds don't fly
Look down into that other street as it shows its face in the un-
    godly hour

Then turn on a light, and hear a sound from something beside
    the window
Of your dream

And come along its beauty like a ladder stretching straight into
    the door which you saw

Between car graves, between these always present artificial lights

That blossom in your hatred hour

Heave some great sound from the depths of the earth, latch on
    like love and always

Destroy what ever, destroy what ever

Weakens days of rain and misted shores gasping with faces

Tomorrow the train, some car or bus
Leaves and there will be a tray with some empty cup
Which you will fight hard with not to drink it because
Of the voice of unreason

Still woods
Broken sound
Love
Streets with ghosts
Train clattering
Bells of God
Nothing.

To Wonder

I bought some candles today
I lit them with my hands, and

They burn cheerfully behind me on the counter.

I look into them, there are two of them, straight and undisturbed by
  the late October wind

Small flames, small hearts in this room.

And there is a man talking in silence

On a spinning machine just by the window

And there are lights fading away behind a sign just in view

And there is a woman I just spoke to that reminded me of something

I watched in a movie long ago

Within me grow gentle veins like the teardrops of a waterfall of
  feelings

Just outside the mist of the pounding water, I see something

And feel it on my cheek, the old touch of melancholy as I turn away

In the dusk by the waterfall

And sometimes I wonder

What the nights will be like

When I have children who are sleeping by a window

Their gentle eyes a sign

And I wonder when I leave this small dwelling

If I will remember what I saw on this night

If I will remember how

In time

To wonder.

Leaves of Trees

You rode in silence over the road
After some great music you composed
Left signs in the leaves between your fingers
In some other morning

I can't come back

And between this music was a great wrathful watching
That you silenced with the waving of your hand
As though through several moments you commanded
The truth inside

A bough of love for you
A strand of truth
A latticed shadow for you
My friend the earth

And through what you said, I brought some other things with me
    that day
In a car filled with roses, in a song filled with the road, and I

Began to remember

And sometimes between the cracks of leaves on your face
A song destroys the lines so carefully placed there by your own
    body and it bursts open
The song bursts open your face and some powerful meaning
    cracks lines in it

So that it is ugly and beautiful

But before I go, I want to show you
Some other piece of music that you wrote
That you didn't know about
That I kept secret within the velvet folds of my heart

It was a poignant and descriptive designation
Of flushed and silent lives
Begging for paper to write their names

I can't understand it, but the music
Like dry dying leaves of trees

Makes seeds for tomorrow, and the sky, if it was in your mind

Is a frothing crystal-green ocean of beginning

Once moved by a song.

Red Hope

Please don't tell them
As you hide out under your blanket sheet in the harsh wind under
    the office building
As though you were children

Don't give any bright sparkling gifts away to those that creep
With
A half-moved other lover in the beginning of your dying day

Don't tell them about your revolution, so small that it
Breaks away the dying day
Puts your dreams in a loving way
Warms your heart with the end of childhood dreams dying so grace-
    fully in one cloudy dream

The clouds rush by you and you lose yourself in them as you are
    lifted, lifted up into
The waking heaven

As you look from your tent which you could have made as a child
    but you are not one

There is a desperate breathing so real that it grips you and you may die

Like a shoe muddied as it runs away from a penciled in amount on a
    check
On a pathway to your cloudy dreams

267

Red hope
Comes in
And in an instant glimpses
This field where weird flowers grow
And you know
My dear friend
That you are lost.

So before the men come down from the office building
And see that you are a fool, and say
Back To Work!

Take that man's hand beneath the tent who could have been your
    friend, when you were a little
Girl
Who could have been a childhood friend
But only a friend

And say something meaningful before someone else comes along
    and takes away your heart

And chews it up beneath the Serendipitous Train Conductor
    Platform of Calamity and Excitement

You are not going away.

Dress in Blue

The guards are coming down
Sing low upon the wind
The concrete laughter of the sound
Bring happiness on wind

There is no frequent sound
To make you want the loudness
Of my previous heart
So coy with madness

I believe in the winter of the day
I believe in that down turned way
There are lyrically singing streets
Down along that way

And they passed me by, with gleam in eye
Into the quaking dream
They brought to me with dream's seed
The beginning of the day

Ever you find a piece of sky
Hanging on the lee

Ever you find my heart so kind
Then bring it back to me

I cherish the way you move your lips
Not in that way
You misunderstand me, then I slip
Along barricades made of the drug of time

That sprinkle the sun with blackness
And cheerfully dress in blue
And love the way you caress

That ocean, that wickedness in you

I combine some other lofty choruses
And tie them up with string

I walk down upon leaves brown
And listen for your singing

But it was never about me, no
It was never too far to go

To where lilies play and frost stays

Among a golden throe

Long Ago

I can breathe on the pristine wind of another basking monument
That with a stone-glass eye returns for me to find

Some breaking of heart

Enunciate for me your dying day
It is changing, and like the weather plays
Along
My
Window-pane

Because I see something you do not see
I look at it from the back, and it runs away
It doesn't breathe, but rather cries
That you've turned away completely

And some changing of concrete stairs
Brings my love within a hair
Of the place where you could find it, fairly

Gone this soaked evening

I bring down to the river
Pieces of some moonlit serenade

And it descends like water into my grave

Oh! But I have but one to save

That is the one I left with pain bereft

So long ago
So long, ago.

And what you whisper in her ear
What you tell her, this I fear

Is that it is what you hold greatly dear

A crusted face of sadness, that

With you
With me

Climbs a seven-limbed tree and speaks for
Your favored lingering words
Upon a clock returning

Yesterday

I can't feel the place for you
You have to find it, and then come to tell me
How wonderfully you stopped the bleeding

Score out a story, then, and relate it to your
Familiars as they corral around the dying fire
And in shaded timbre huskily berate your fathers

I know now why you walked away
I knew that it was something to do with
The coiling breath of another child-like eye
Stopping in the middle of your sleep

Truth can't be found here, no you've looked in the wrong place
I know the wind

Is gone, again

Sacredly rescinding into mad and quiet desire

The soft mask you wear when you walk into the room

Is like a song that never ends

Unless you push it down your mouth and feel

The watching of tomorrow

I cannot find the center, even when
You show it to me

It moves away and does not speak a word

As it walks out the door

I know that there is something truthful for you to find

Yet it is yesterday

Down below there are golden majesties
That speak with the coolness of April water
And glisten and gleam like the dream you once had
When you awoke to the crows outside your window

And they said nothing, but rather

Watched the tree-felling

Something You Feel

You linger on for a swollen moment
And like the wind you smell the sea
Concentrated on a droplet of silver on a withered flower
You see a reflection of a thousand muted faces

When can you ever come back home
It is new now, and different
Lingering on in the old places like a forgotten glance
And sun streams down in the old unfeeling way

But there must be something more sacred
More dear to your heart that comes here
It is not something that you find in a place beside a window

It is something you feel

When, if you'll remember, did you ever
Feel that the old house, under sacred moonlight
Was ever something that you wanted to feel?

And you break the chains
They fling from your body like waves of light
And they drop to the ground a thousand feet below
So far down that they make no sound

And you look inside that old house, before you turn to go
And you see something in its face, old and pleading
But ready to give you newness in a distant call of hope

And another wing, another day
Floats by and then you say

That this is it

This eternal moment for the now dividing sky

And something crucial belongs to you

Again this hopeful darkened night

You bring it in, you cherish its sweet rosy must

And you believe that this what you could never find

The Watchman

I interacted with a cruel coward
Who told some of his most

Blinding Jokes

And the way that the trees moved around him was in
A solid never moving silent screeching

The wicked lines are drawn
The faithful watching ever
The movement of the dawn
The scratching flight of never

And in the darkest brew
Of all the angels flew
The darkest member of the crew

The watchman

Night glistened in his path
Which he destroyed forever in wrath
And lengthened the hollow laugh

Of the bells remembering

He took upon his staff
The aching darkened math
And with a hope-filled flask

Came to ask us how to dance

What greater kind of loving lie
Can you muster in the sky
What grievance of this passing by

Of death

But there once was in the misty shore
The lonely galloping watching boy
Who always took

My life

The end is coming near
I feel it not so distant
It comes with a piece of bitter cloth

So take
So break
This fragile heart of mine
So wake
So partake

In the end

Sad

If you keep trying to keep
Me alive

It doesn't work sometimes, and then I see
Some cowardly crawling cretin that you never can

Blissfully parched in the ways of the world
Is the beggar bright and clean
Yet he stares and still cares about it
The wintry chalice of Dream

I want to hear you out, my dear
Yet always when I speak it comes out as though you thought I was

Sad

Color it, mix it in
The fragrant lips of a toxic gin
That you gulp down each time you wake

Pray the Lord takes no souls

Sometimes I feel as though with my dying breath
I will say a word

Rummage through, make due
With the mind you are offered
Collect here, collect there
The missing falling coffers

Of the wretchedness which hides you
        From my face
Of the destruction which you wish so dearly
Onto it

Take me home, sweet rose
Take me to where you were born
Take me home, prickly thorn
Never on a brow were you ever worn

And give me a notice
Eviction
And straighten up, act like a grammar-man

When you are in her presence

Can you ever lose me
Can you ever see
That when you touch me with your eyes
That you're killing me

I don't want to go back there
Please take me away

Yet you, my friend
You were always me

Shadow Weep

I let myself die beside
A part of a bell-tower
Showering me with the petals
Of a former life

And I heard them speak
The endings of the shelves
On which I placed a piece
Of wicked shadow weep

I had friends
That sharpened their knives
Against the broken rocks
Of my love

And I waited, waited long
For the bells to prolong
A piece, a strand, a song
Of love that is wrong

Yarn of the Sea

The old man sat against the wind
The stones and the living thread
A whisper faint in broken light
His long beard the sea

And said have I a tale to tell
Of the ancient ships that used to dwell

Inside your wicked land
Inside your wicked land

Destroy what you love
If you want to be like me
Destroy what you love
And toss it in the sea

Blithe, merry, don't you tarry
To bring with me your pity
I don't want any of it
In the whispering shade of jade tree

Long ago, there used to be
A king who had my name

What king?

Chariot Devil

Forbidden times we used to sing
Break fall, rhyme and casket
I can't remember what you danced with

The world can't breathe now, it seems
What did you use to dance with

Love is mine, said a flash of light
From a still painting painter
As you stood smiling beside your sister

Whose name was Dream
Who broke and screamed
The making of your whisper

Carving, carving
The whole world is dying
Elicit for me, you mongers of luck
The sweet taste of that forgotten cup

I brought with me into the desert
A piece of wire and a book with empty pages
So I could dig for sunlight
In the rain

Babbling, blabbing
The witch is cackling
And always rasping at your other door

Spring forth you magic jesters
And quell and quench the begotten qualm
Of danger-making, hair-thin faking
Which passes barely through a TV wall

Wring around
Sing down
Chariot devil
And ascend the wintering frost of the next century

Blossom for the Winter of Our Love

I wanted to give you something of gravity and power
Yet the morning is so far away
Withering within this very hour

Blend and shake and wrestle
The quenching spirit of the morning
For it will kill you
For it will kill you

And all your great magic designs
Spread across the countryside
Designating what is mine
And what you left behind

Tomorrow may come, but tonight
Drink and bring down boughs of delight
So that the savior might
Be driven off for our evening fright

Because of what you once said to me
Fate
 have not forgotten your curious and dark name
Against the whispers of the shadow

But believe that when you leave here
That I will take
And berate your wretched name

To arms, the mighty swelling of the wind
Not so grand in the fading willow tree
Not so lovely in my ear
This touch of melancholy

Blossom for the winter of our love
Take care, and guide your hand
Along the strands that command
My heart

And never fade, and never place
Your head on pillows soft
Until you see, until you breathe
The wisdom of tonight

All the People I Know

All the people I know
Pass me by in a parade
And I sit and watch from my window
Where I know if I jump out and join them, I will die

Sometimes I wonder what's deep inside me
Then I realize that it's a butterfly made of glass
That I put inside my soul when I was seven years old
And haven't found since

This morning I was happy
Tonight I am sad

There is a wondrous delight
Made of paper lanterns and love
That I need sometime beside the glowing river
Of the rotund of sacred myths I cling to like a child

Oh keeper of the healing garb
Woman, so kind and warm
I need you to come with me
I need you to protect me from harm

I sit in my castle all day
In the West wing
And the sun slants through the room
Displaying all fine things

Yet there is something missing
Among piles of gold
There is something missing here
It is respite for my soul

Can you give me what I want
Never, not at all
Can you give me what I want
As I despair in the West Wing Hall

And founder to my sleeping place
And wish that I could take my face
Away from fire that lights its way
Across my eyelids blistering

Someone love me, I desperately say
As birds fly down from the peaks of gray
And bring me to my final days
Without love

Bring me a chalice
Of the past
So I may toast to what could have been
Had things gone differently

Tonight I think of you my love
When you've all but forgotten me
Tonight, tomorrow, eternity
The days when I'll love thee.

I Think Something Big Will Happen

I think something big will happen
And then I see the rows of clouds
Passing me by with eyes and breath
Like make-believe monsters

And they smile and offer a hand, smoke
Steaming from their mouths, and I
Think murder

But before I take you down
This pathway down 'round
The chasm of my heart
I will pray

To pray is to give up in yourself

I went before my master
And asked him for change
Of time

Do not suffer, do not weep
Do not long for days to keep
Do not bring for me, my sweet
My beckoned witchcraft sleep

I cannot ever see what sort of blame has felled me
So that I can bring my golden keys that unlock secrets
And doors to your cruelty which I beg for on the floor
And pray that a solo chorus will end my hope

For when, within
The break of day begins
This is when, my friend
That hearts refuse to bend

And give you endless grief
And strike you to the streets
Where you can find your keep
Amongst the wondering water of peace

Vindicate and corrupt the sacred blistering
And turn it into a forward-pointing star

And give it to your maker and close the door

Create for Me

Create for me
In those beautiful halls
Where laughter is like water

A small fragment
Of that jewel you call love
That passes so easily
From eye to eye

Where have you hid it
Down below, down below
You placed it in the river
So it flows easily out of my reach

And what I have done
Comes quickly to their eyes
In another city down the river
Where my love is their prize

Inside the Heaven Room

A man alone on lasting tears
Kissed away by heaven's breath
Came down from the listening fear
And began to dream of heaven blessed

Fueling his fire a waking dream
Against his eyelids sleeping
He dreamt of his old and ancient, that seemed
To pass before his eyelid

The ones that came before him, spoke
The old family he never knew
The old bearers of hardened yoke
The smiling pathways he never knew

They gathered 'round his quivering lid
And said, Get up, for the hour
Is late and your bones will turn to sour
Never fear, for I am watching

They watched him sleep, and travel far
Through destiny and all its shapes
Through misery and between its quake
The mystic shores of yearning

They spoke nothing, and let him float
Through dreams and lost thoughts
They brought him from the toil of time
And gave him each their blessing

The sweeping of the ancient myth
Only seen in dreams
What can you hide from heaven's grip?
A piece, they said, of dreams

There once was a song, they said
With melody so true
There once was a song, they said
For me and you

But as the corners of his eyes
Began to see into themselves
And on their corners, a thousand wells
Of an endless prism of gasping light

What rooms, they brought him, said they'd find
What rooms and colors masking
The brilliant and direct course through
A scene of heaven's making

In heaven, there is a room
Where you keep all your favorite loves
In heaven, they keep this darkened room
Alone in a sea of white

You have your maps, your long lost love
Against the walls as paintings
You have your sleep, and have your thrall
Of the thousands of trinkets invisible

They tinkle as you walk
Suspended as the air
They bring with them, a piece of chalk
To carry you up the tarrying stair

And with you, unseen at last
Are all your forbears true
They sit and laugh and mock and rue
The colors that are untrue

But one last thing, he spoke again
Against the walls of the room
There is a canvas for her face
Inside the heaven room

There is a canvas for her face

Inside that heaven room

The Passing of Midnight on Halloween

The crass father beamed at his chosen children
And spells became like the moon

There was something deep inside that she wrote
But you left it on the parlor table, leaving with all the various
    golds that you

Gambled away with, when these certain golds were more pristine
    in you than

What could ever be made into a stake, what could ever be made
    into the likeness of them

What ever could be made into the sickling harvests

I knew a few spell-casters joyful unbidden women who wandered
    around my sleeping place

I knew that it was then that I was not alone, again, ever

The fearful watching never
The flight of Christ gone forever

Within the mocking door

Within the parlor's sentries
That I paid off with some souls scraped from the floor

With some hidden wondrous chambers left bare from haunted
    yore, I plead that the

Witches with me were here to take from me more,

Take from me more, these olden gifts, these salvaged ships, these
    wrecked on the shore

Take away your stake, doorman, I have wiped the floor with your
    ashes and you sleep

I kept matches and books with them for your end-time favorite
    implore

And nothing else wept with me while I mused and beguiled
    them, fought and derided them

Laughing with me on the floor

Laughing at the buried Christ chamber door.

There is no mystery in the moon, it's just a favor
That you wished for when you begged for saviors
When you were smitten with the shatterglass calamity blood

It rises in you and pitches itself to high notes alongside the meters
    and the machines which

Explode at your touch, because you walked into the choir cham-
    ber, touched the machine that

Measured your heart and you broke every dial, the glass shatter-
    ing to the floor, and eventually

Like the place where they dropped the bomb, turned into ash which
     collected around your heart

Until some favor, blistering danger, you rose up and said more:

Goodbye, trespasser, goodbye Union jack, I never kept a place for you

Just made a grave for you, passing by the ever door,

I made instead a name of it
The plastic wedding cake of it
The children laughing came for it
And cast it through the door

I wept I kept I stayed for it, but I never prayed to it, I never made it
     a costume that I wore

Tomorrow, as the hour strikes 12:04

I wrote a line that curved with time, then left me like a shade of yore,

It ended and the words upended and a bump from the edge of the
     pale empty kitchen door,

Which was not the same but instead frightened the tame into
     thinking that it was nothing more,

Then ghost goblin smacking ghoul I took and painted on the floor,
     again, with me, too crazed to

See

When the day was done I emptied rum and collapsed its entirety in
     my chest,

Where I could save it for someone else's more

Printed in Great Britain
by Amazon